TOM FALLON

THE CHANGE OF THE CENTURY

THE MAN ON THE MOON

THE MAN ON THE MOON

The Change of the Century

> THE MAN ON THE MOON

TOM FALLON

A Transition Book

Library of Congress Catalog Card Number: 87-90496

ISBN 0-9616146-3-3

Publication of this book was made possible, in part, by a grant from the Maine Arts Commission.

Published by
small-small Press/
CHARTENG WORKSHOP
226 Linden St.
Rumford ME 04276

First Edition

For Jacqueline Thibodeau, an equal
partner in the creations.

Time is the greatest innovator.

Francis Bacon

*What I write, as I have said before,
could only be called poetry because
there is no other category
in which to put it.*

Marianne Moore

CONTENTS

THE MAN ON THE MOON is a work-in-progress.
"Improvisation #2" will be continued; another WYSIWYG,
and perhaps 2 more Improvisations will be created, to
synthesize the 20th Century
literary revolution.

TO THE READER

No, the 20th Century revolution of the arts didn't begin in the 20th Century - the revolution began with the development of Aristotlean science - the change in human consciousness which sought answers to the nature of the world from objective reality rather than from the subjective myth-making imagination.

And then during the Italian Renaissance, the return of Greek culture from the darkness of the Middle Ages stimulated the further development of this objective-reality philosophy, directing intellectuals to observe the real, or material, world, to more accurately define the world's reality. So mythmaking became an activity of the past, myths preserved only by religious institutions, and the source of their creation also "dried up" for human society.

The invention of the telescope and the microscope revealed worlds previously invisible to the human intellect and encouraged a revolutionary speculation about the nature of the world's reality: a feverish investigation of materiality through observation mounted in society's intellectual circles to gain a knowledge of the "true" reality.

Inventions also began to change the way the majority of the people thought about the world as well as the way they moved and worked in their daily lives: the social environment was revolutionized by the many new self-propelled machines that came into existence.

Science sounded a "death knell" to sensual beauty "in the old sense", and replaced this with "the truth" of the new hidden material world. The revelation of a different layer of reality by scientific investigations, the destruction of the old and real natural world so easily interpreted by the senses, also stimulated a search for a different reality by artists, with the consequent invention of different techniques and new art forms to express the "new reality".

Of course, it is now a cliche to write that the investigations of Sigmund Freud, Charles Darwin, Albert Einstein and other scientists completed the revolution of the new thought-direction in human society's consciousness. So, too, William Carlos Williams, Gertrude Stein, e. e. cummings, Ezra Pound, T. S. Eliot, among others, from the same philosophical base, questioned the traditional literary form and forged a new poetic thought-direction termed "modern", which helped to create the aesthetic concepts for the new human social consciousness.

The same revolutionary change - so much more appealing to the ordinary imagination - took place in the plastic arts as "modern" art was created by the exploration of Cezanne, Monet, Picasso, Duchamp, Kandinsky, Moore, Smith, and many others.

So it is that a literary revolution took place in the 20th Century just as a plastic arts revolution did - and although that literary revolution in form is recognized today as a radical departure from traditional prose and poetic form, it is not yet clearly understood for the departure it truely is - the first stage in the development of a new literary category. The possibility for a new literary category has been pioneered by the fathers of the modern movement - the freedom now exists for a new literary category to be created.

So be it...!

TOM FALLON
Rumford - 1987

PREFACES

13

First Preface

Rumford Falls *Times*
Wed., May 29, 1985

Dear Editor:

Papermaking is a special industry because paper has played
such a significant role in the advancement of human civilization.

Paper is made here in Rumford by people who have spent their
lives in the paper mill - by sons and daughters, brothers and
sisters, by nieces and nephews, and by grandsons and grandaughters.

The paper made by the people from the area towns of Byron,
Carthage, West Peru, Dixfield, Mexico, Bethel, as well as Rumford,
is used for entertainment, intellectual and business purposes in
the advancement of our present civilization which has implanted
artificial hearts in human beings and rocketed to the surface
of the moon.

The other day at the Boise Cascade Rumford paper mill, a new
and special grade of paper was being made for the first time.
Everyone involved in this paper making operation was working very
hard to make the unfamiliar grade of paper right so that it
would meet the customer's strict specifications. The intensity
of the people making the paper pointed out the pride of the
papermakers in the mill.

Yet, how many of those who work in the Boise Cascade paper
mill are "born" papermakers - or have been schooled specifically
for paper making and its allied sciences? Very, very few. But
these unschooled papermakers were making this special grade of
paper as if they were "born" papermakers - they loved the challenge
of making this difficult grade of paper!

Yes, papermaking is a singular industry of human civilization -
and the economic foundation of Rumford, Maine - we should all be

14

proud of the paper makers working and sweating in the Boise
Cascade mill of our small town - for the "ratrace" of this
modern paper manufactory is the foundation of human civilization.

Second Preface

So it is, you
    are probably today
                heading into space -

    away from the earth
            that place on which you were born,
    away from - as far as
            we human beings

                            know -
        that novel place
            moving in space
                    we named earth -
        away from the life
        of single cells
                fish, frogs
            scorpions, beavers, deer
                and
                    elephants

            as well as *homo sapiens*
        that novelty of creation,

the only life on

earth

and in space - in the far-reaching space

of the universe - with the moving, ever
turbulent
and enormous galaxies
in
the humanly unimaginable size of the universe -

so that you will soon
be leaving
the solar system
in your spacecraft,
to see
as far back
into the created
universe as time
allows -

to search also

for other intelligent beings
on some yet undiscovered
planet -
in the few thousand years of
your intellectual
history, you are here
away
from the darkness of caves
in the darkness of
outer space

brought here into the unknown
by your quizzical nature - however

much still
            misunderstood (why am I here, what am I,
    still
            an unknown world) - "as it is written"
on paper
            on manufactured mass-produced books, words
                                        read
                by all humans on earth
            minds spurred
                        by ideas,
                            new questions on paper,
                                new
                                        answers -
searching,
  searching creation
                for knowledge and understanding
of creation -
            you travel, today, near
                        the speed of light away

                                    from Pluto

                    into the unknown -
                    a daring

            infinitely small, living
                        creature
                    in the limitless

        novel
                universe .   creation

Third Preface

                              so *that*
  i   am   uncertain   about   myself   ..

     i walk   with   uncertainty , as if

         almost
     I   hadnt   learned   to walk   very well,

& people
            (in
Bartash's store, watch i walk across the main street))
   are   watcheng   me   because
                                  I   showed

                                        my

                  uncertainty   as

       i walked /i   felt   in   my   bodie
                      my

                          unCertain ness:

          my feet
on the   cement sidewalk are   placed   one   in
                  front ov   the   other   ,insecurely ,
                                    InmyAer ,,,

so, out of the trees the caves. the animal. out, of burrows,

    The alphabet. S K Y   -   *T R E E* .

18

printeng, before

before the print-PAPER.!

          -continouslie   w/me

then,   (IN MI MIND!)

how

to   conquer dethe :

the mind's

conquest/verbal

"contest"   with   deathe

                    (darknese)..

       o   n   Pa   pp   e   r

change the worlde
change the worlde
change the worlde
change the worlde
change the worlde
change the worlde
change the worlde
change the worlde
change the worlde
change the worlde
change the worlde
change the worlde
change the worlde   (human *spirit* "strange. . ."

            universe.&   my human

                      unsertantee,,

    [*walk* ak-ros   Congres   strete)..

IMPROVISATION #1

An Ordinary Man, Moving (on the earth) 1986

1.

Christ I hate this shift.
"Bye! I'm leavin' now," I called, shutting the front
door. *The night's dark.*
The door opened. "You got your lunch," Jackie asked.
"Of course," I answered, turning to her as I went down
the front walk. "See you in the mornin'." *The house was
lit up.*
I walked down the front walk with my lunch basket hooked
over my forearm. *The night air warm. I should be going to
sleep not to work.* I felt the warm air. *Nice.*
Walk. *No: no: no. Hard to sleep at night before work:
I hate this shift. I hate. Shut down, I shut down (mind).
And again.*
I saw the night sky alight, a white orange glow, the
lights around the paper mill. I heard the high-pitched
whine of the machinery as one sound – in the warm night air.
Dark. Walk. The house alight, door closed. Front
walk under my foot, my feet. I walk. *Feet.*
*You got your lunch. (Think, [create]...) Goddamit
I hate this shift.* On the front walk, I saw the white
orange glow and I heard the high-pitched whine in the night
air. *See, then, and hear; open up the (creative) mind...it
exists.*
I walk. *No. Open.* Moveng.
*Money, money: the paper mill: I like the money.
(Creation...[always].)...creation. Create the world.*
Walking, I am, on my feet, down the front walk.

2.

A.

Into the paper mill I took part of a manuscript, what
I had written, and typed, today, a projected part of this
creation, from my life: to have the words, and their total
form, with me. If I could not reread them because the paper
testing load was too heavy, I'd at least have them near me,
to pick up at times, to absorb into my unconscious "depth",
in this way, for re-creation, re-forming, "fulling", fitting
in with what else was already generating in my mind, or to
absorb and probe with this part more parts of the whole
creation from my moving unconscious - to keep the creation
in my mind, to hold creation in my mind as a necessity, to
make creation a reality for my sometimes laggard self. In
my lunch basket, made of interwoven wood slats like a picnic
basket, although half that size, unpainted until I had
painted it green - not the Boise "puke" green - I had the
biggest size lunch basket made so I could bring notes,
manuscripts and books, even hardcover if necessary, yes -
with my lunches for work - to keep my conscious-unconscious
together with the part-creation, keep the creativity moving,
simply by feeling near the creative piece, creative thing,
prompting my own creation - to prompt my awareness of myself
as a creation - my own living creation reality - keep my
self open to my creation - unnerved within that creative
process - near the source - near, the consciousness, unconsciousness, the uncertain movement back and forth, opening
between with the uncertainty of that transitory, fluctuating
state, a reality the creation, the living, the anxiety a
necessity, the risk, the conscious kept off-balance by the
strong unconscious, continuously the flow of the unconscious,
as I "courted" the "death", the end of consciousness in the
unconscious - to create, to be, part of, near, as often as

possible - creation, the whole, living, the universe -
creativity, in my lunch basket, "the force" in the Quality
Control Lab - necessity, and fear in me, Tom, human being,
part, small, of creation, universe, a necessity, to live
fully near the source of creation, the creation - near death
of my self continuously - giving my self up - for the creation -
no value - being only - and my death - self-sacrifice -
"burning" up to know creation - (love creation, know the
"burning, unbelievable" joy in the, that, creation) - of no
practical value but to be - see, with the "inner mind", the mind
of creation, my whole, pairing with the whole creation,
seeing and knowing the source, creation "present" in me -
losing my self in the creation, transcending my smaller self
yet my larger self knowing the creation and its source -
energy - self "expanded", knowing, "seeing" the full universe,
creation - in my lunch basket, I walked with the basket over
my forearm, the front walk, creation, there - summer night
air - me, perfection. My lunch basket was heavy tonight
because I had a history of papermaking by Dard Hunter, book
hardcover, in it - heavy on my forearm. *My feet on the walk.*
Here. The creation, being. (I). *Whole..*create.

I took the working manuscript to the paper mill in my lunch
basket: to keep in my mind. (I did not know where I'd fit
it, how it could change, if I would change it, how it would
effect my conscious thought, being.) I put it into my
basket, three folded pieces of paper typewritten on the
Olivetti 45D. *Thought* - part of my self, creation, in the
paper mill. white orange glow:
transcendent, in my lunch basket - so

                              then,

the words, on paper, I brought into the mill:

with feet
        on solid-ness
earth, & the moon
also -

    the moon away

up
  in the sky - or, earth,
the earth
    'in the sky
  away,
     there -

  there it is: I·was
  born
    on earth

in space,
 in the universe, so
      return
  to earth from
  the moon,
    from
      space...

speeding through space in
Apollo spacecraft

                              toward
                              earth
            from

                    the moon

        (i looked at the earth as we approached)...

    ...moveng toward earth ,   thru space
         (in the solarsystem)

    i was moveng toward the earth   from/ the moon-

                              Space

                (earlier today
                 i walked
                      on the moon,)

                    i // was // born /// onthe // earth .
                                              there
         "Shit, I ain't workin' in a paper mill to make paper -
    I work in this mill to make money - I don't give a tinker's
    shit about makin' paper - I don't give a tinker's shit about
    the company neither cuz the company doesn't give a shit about
    me! I gotta eat and feed my horses so I work for good ole
    Oxford. Salary don't give a shit about makin' paper neither
     - they're in it for the money jus' like I am - money, money,
    money, they talk about - their investments everywhere - and
    that's the game in this old paper mill. Thursday's my day
    of the week, payday. Hell, I used to cut wood on my own and

"sell it to good ole Oxford - I banged up my skidder and lost
a horse and the bank wouldn't swing me another skidder, the
bastards - so I got in the woodyard here and I'm happy as a
pig in shit! I wouldn't work on those fuckin' paper machines
for five thousand dollars a week - those guys down in the mill
are nuts - I worked there for three weeks when I first came
in the mill - no more! Naw, I don't give a tinker's shit about
paper unless it's the green kind, y'know money, money, money!
Papermakin's jus' another way to make a livin' that's all -
it's just a job!"
                    No Odysseus.
                    No Maximus -
                    no Paterson.
                    Not Dublin.
                    Not Brooklyn:
                    not Europe.

No Odysseus. Not Maximus. No, not Paterson. Not Dublin;
not Brooklyn. No not Europe. Tom Fallon: Rumford - America.

I'm not Ishmael - no, nor Odysseus - or is it Ulysses? No
Maximus, nor Paterson can I be accused of: just Tom - that
simple - Tom; the surname, Fallon - our 1st American Fallon
a "night-soiler" in Cambridge Mass - no myths surrounding me
here in America: none. Let's not have the myth, nothing
supernatural. A human being. My action. My mind's action.
Opinions, the writing - let's have this, OK? No gods as a
metaphor - no, no metaphor, let's end the metaphor - and all
that other poetry stuff... State clearly - "no poetry" -
state, then, "Tom Fallon must create something else. What
literary form, then? structure, should be created?" (Above
all, don't follow "the crowd".) Let's clearly underline the

extinction, the uselessness, of poetry, now, as a literary
form - create anew, OK? It is possible...*to invent*...
                              And Reta

                                            the woman fat,
                                                  mother
                                        always her yap
                                knew all Rumford's
                                              biznus
                                      dammit, especially
                        "bad stuff" (personal) mother-in-law
                        her holiday family meals, "knocked
                                              herself out"
                              baking for days, children and
                          grandchildren all together, she
                              "mother hen" happy - her
                                        family, together,
above anything else,
family -
        here in Rumford - she's dead. (Pop. 8,000)
                                  She lived next door and
                                  used to sit and play
                          solitaire, look out the window so she
                                  could see everyone who came
                                              up the walk.
                                              Isabel,
                                          still-born
                                            Jackie
                                            Jimmy
                                            Jerry
                                  Johnny, died as a boy
Ginger
                                          and Julie,
      her children, all born in Rumford, she was, still in the town.
FAMILY -   *she believed in people, as they are*...
                                  human   home.
    HUMAN..

B.

    I could hear water flowing in the small brook, across
the street, Bean Brook, in the night air, its soft noise
in the night air, and our trip to Auburn this afternoon,
my mother, Jackie and I, came into my consciousness, the
drive from Bethel to Norway, the pass through the village
of Locke Mills, just outside the village the lakes on either
side of the road - the lakes in the trees - pass the lakes
with the trees in full green, remember this place at its
most perfect, leaves a light yellow -

                  the most beautiful
                      place
                              on earth, for me

                         the highway - no
                           super highway -
                              passing through
                                  the woods
 passes
           between the lakes, the water
                        on both sides
           of the road
        so that
            in the fall
                    trees
              with leaves changed
                      color,
        some a light yellow,
    these leaves
           on a promontory
              of the highway

     seem to float in air

over the water and

            driving the car,

              my eyes pass

                  quickly

        back and forth

              between the sides

   of the highway

one lake

     to another

        on each side of me, slowing

        the car

           to see, feel this

              beauty

     around the highway, of

  the water

      moving slightly in the sun's light,

      small waves

         touched by light,

      white tipped waves'

        reflecting,

          moving

     brilliant light

    with the grey-blue water

in the distance

   on both sides, hills, treed, evergreens

            loom

    and

  I see

    the water

       on both sides of me as I slow,

     pass

                the lakes
                            around me,
                            around the land, trees, in the light,

        come upon
                the waters from out of the village
                            of no consequence, light dotting the
                            highway, shadows
                                        moving
                                over the glass-steel car,

                        the ponds

                                    beside the highway — and in
                        the middle,
                        between the ponds, in a suddenly unreal
                                            world — to me —

                        I am

                                        between on the narrow
                                        strip of highway
                    surrounded by
                        a nature now
                        significant

        my consciousness
                    on the highway,
                                    the unconscious
                    the lakes
                            water
                        on either side of

                    the road
                                        water
                in nature, and
                come upon suddenly, as
                    my discovery of
                        my unconscious -

                                its vitality -
            fulfillment - is discovered -

        so that I love this place on earth
            the earth floating
                            on water, an uncertainty
                    because it represents my - (no, I did

                    not know this fact
                        when I first was struck by
                                the place'
                                    significance) -

                    my intellectual, creative
                                        life
            the unconscious, the unconscious, the unconscious

                    I must sink into my self,
                            into this reality
                    see, as I do now
                                the lakes, the water
                        on
            either
                    side of the road as I ride - almost riding
        on
            the water - ride in the glass-steel car, the highway

my self   held up by the water
the earth itself

held on water, held on water
surrounded by water:
the depths

here

in the sun-shadowed light -
summer -

my creation   my creation

This place
           as no other place I've yet seen.   Close
              to Rumford

      and while, at one time, the
      river banks of the Androscoggin in Rumford,
                        the pond and dirt roads
                           at Roxbury Pond,
      the roadside across from the house,
              my garden
                       were satisfying, now, this
                                              place

       just outside Locke Mills
                 recreates

           only   my mind's movement -
represents   my creation, and I look for a camp to rent
for the summer
           to be near the water, the crossing

                                    highway at Locke
                                            Mills,
                                    the water's depth

DEEP   THE UNKNOWN   TEEMING
                                    WITH LIFE
                    AND ITS VARIETY

    CREATION   INVISIBLE   YET BENEATH   THE WATER

                        WATER

                                    A FAMILIAR,LIFE

                                            WITH RISK, YES
INTO THE WATER,   INTO THE WATER

                                    TO DROWN

                                                AND RETURN
    YES, RETURN

            WITHOUT FAIL   TO CAPTURE
                                    CREATIVITY

                                                THERE

                    IN WATER,

                                    THE WATER

THE WATER
     DEPTH
again, in my mind, I drive away from Locke Mills
  the two ponds, the water, the water
            in the sun of the fall afternoon,
                     in the sunlight of the summer
                             afternoon.
     And, Bean Brook, flowing, in the summer night.....
  water
      noise...

this, most beautiful, this
                   most beautiful - water, on both
      sides
         of the road - light - water - floating
two
   huge
      pools of water   in the light
                      passeng

               3.

            Mother-in-law Reta is gone now
              I am here   her daughter
              Jackie, too, alive:

             Mother-in-law Reta is gone
        (the house empty, windows unlighted)
             I am here   her daughter
              Jackie, too, alive, 46
                years of life...
            her death, the windows
           of her unlighted house,
                 home,

empty, no human

and, next door, windows lighted
the family Fallon alive
her daughter,
the eldest
Thibodeau
which means the days are now numbered
for us
I, am the oldest at 50
the half-century of living
human
I am
Reta died in the night, gone

before anyone knew in the hospital, waking
the big woman, mother, at 1 AM,
her leg feeling good
her leg feeling good
she remarked
to the nurse, and at 3 AM

dead
in her sleep

and the telephone woke us
up, Jackie
gasped,
her sister Ginger calling
from the hospital
Rumford Community, our hospital,
so Reta died, mother, and Jackie

went to the hospital, for a
few final minutes with her mother - yes,
gone.   Windows, in her house, home
no longer will be lighted.

by Reta, significant, mother, I
fought with
— two big shots —
bossy, told to "go fly a kite", ate at many
of her family gatherings, her family
for Christmas, Thanksgiving, Mother's Day, her whole
she "knocked herself out" cooking for, her
sons Jimmy and Jerry, her daughters Jackie
Ginger and Julie, her
grandsons, grandsons finally Tommy, Alex and Kenrick,
Patrick, Johnny, and grandaughters, Mary, Kathy, Becky,
Deirdre, Hope, Jennifer and Jill, Jessica
and Amanda
myself, Jackie's husband, Yutta Jimmy's wife and
Jerry's wife
Nancy

Eddie,
Ginger's husband, Dwight
Julie's husband, all in
Rumford but Dwight
and Julie who were in
Locke Mills 30 miles away —
to eat at the family gatherings — poor Albert
the father
gone —
he could cook meat better drunk than
anyone sober — the family
Reta's family, her substance, sustenance
everyone in Rumford she grew up
with a family
her reality,
family
She
dead, no
consciousness, as

I see
my own mind,

the consciousness
to die,
end
end
clearly now
I am alone on the "promontory" of life's last
years
I must think
about
necessity,
the necessity creation's
made I do not
understand
the end of time for individual
life, me,
and my wife, Jackie
with "numbered"

days,
we are together,
end, end

end of consciousness - me -
this part of the Thibodeau family, Fallon, (with Jackie
[Thibodeau]) -
history,
definitely
gone
so that my eyes will no longer see as my mind
has seen, known, up until now
feeling human,
in the sense of frail
vulnerable, vulnerable
as I

                                                        have
not
        before felt - windows, in "that" grey house,
                            in this night, now not lighted,
                                and never again
                                    will be, by Reta

                            Mahala Thibodeau (Boyle)
        and my sadness, exists, for her, because she was
                                        real -
                    understanding life as I did not, now
                                know, could not
                                    know her
                            life by that first word
                                of her death,
                            knowledge, understanding
            for a human being, a very fat, short woman, always
        gabby, over-eating, sometimes so "viscious" her gossip, yet
    her trust in God, her love of her children, of her family
                                        gathered
                        around her as often as possible,
                    her frail, human life, her giving,

                only the silence exists as future, the word
                                in
        that silence, here, only my human consciousness and my
                                    ignorance:
                                    the end.
                                    Only,

                            from earth
            in the universe, the great unknown universe
                    that human,   word :   in the silence.
                                        life once -
                        Death:
                        Death: in my future, soon

                    as I knew when a little boy

                                    nothingness:
COMPLETE EXTINCTION
of my mind   (and I don't know any
                    way out of this extinction -
unless God the creator exists -)
                                              Reta
        human, real   gone   ..   simply -
          a warmth   I do not have,
and, yet   in Jackie (her daughter) I can see
                                    the woman dead.

to sit side by side with Jackie, now
     on the couch, watching television after supper, and
                          holding hands, 46, 50,
                    a man and a woman, human,
                    with each other, mother and
                                        father

              with only 3 children now at home, 4 left home
          comfortable, at times, with
                    each other, holding hands at home:

I WILL DIE.   a man of cold intellect, ambition,
and, I will find out/ find out
    perhaps,   what form
                        I'll take of an individual self
                    the human (dying) self, can it
in reality   - be - collected   into

                a "living" unconscious of
                the universe . all, life

in the   *a priori*   creative whole state - after death
     some kind of metamorphosis, I cannot now imagine as I

never have "imagined"
the universe/earth,creation –

Reta,   Reta,   dead.
                human, ...

(Sunday, now..

4.

and I should be going, walking
from the house, to work   in the night
summer air, tonight   to test paper in
the Lab, the one room   walk
through the Time Office and
pick up my time card – walk through
the yard, across railroad tracks past the
steam plant smoke pouring into
the black sky
the mill yard buildings lit
by orange white lights harsh
into the Kraft Mill basement
through "black ash alley" and
the old brick of the Kraft Mill, the
rusted iron
circular stairway up to the Beater Room noise
through/by #4 paper machine
wet end/stock moving on the moving wire
up into the first dryers through the
noise   the second dryer section, the paper drying
and

winding up into a wide roll   take
            a right at the dry end of the PM into
            the Core Room and the air-conditioned
        Lab, a right   to work, but I

                        5.

                                            Stand, then
                                        to turn & look at,
                                            the house
                                            there
                                        in the night
                                        summer air
                                        & once,
                                        this place

                                    lighted windows;
                                        Home.
                                Family: my, family,
                                        in the House.
                                Our, family, children
                                                there
so that my mother, in the house - not here - secure
                            Mother   and son,
                                        the world secure
                                        My

        & that day it rained - familiar
            rain - rained hard more than a day - 2 boys
            inside the camp at Taylor Pond/Auburn
                                    Spring, mother
                    to find me something

42

                        to do/ the boys   Mommy: "let's learn
"your letters"   but I knew the letters at 8, "no,
    "you have to do them right"
                        so, a little boy unwilling
to learn what he knew
                        sat at the oak
                    old, round table, Mommy
making the 1st a̲ - "OK, now try to make
    your a̲ just like mine - OK?"
                                I made the letter a̲ under
                            my mother's letter a̲
    "No. Look, now, at my a̲ - here, see how
        it curves here & yours doesn't?"
                                        I saw
                                        it, then
                        "Here, make another one now"   so
                        that I made another one,
                            an a̲,

                        looking, comparing the 2 letters,
                                saw, *no*

    different   made
another letter a̲ painstakingly,
    she was right,   she said "Draw the letter..."

        I showed her my letter a̲ - heard, rain on roof
        "Good, that's better, OK now,
                            the b̲ - "
                    & she made the letter b̲ for me *to copy*
so I tried to copy it, but
    the/MY, letter b̲
                    wasn't the same: tried again
                to make the letter,
                    make the b̲ better - "Good"
                so I worked on my letters, one / by / one
(because Mommy believed in my mind)
            to make the letters right - tho I knew
                how to make the letters -   *to make*

crafteng   letters,   these
  letters   Important, *makeng*
            the letters
                        in my mind,
          as perfect
            (in my mother's warmth:
                        Belief/perfection

          "Right", she said
                    in the camp, rain, the
                rain falling
                            down roof, mother
      my familiar/secure, in camp - discipline she
            "make letters - *learn*.."
              home, mother - lights, the warmth
                    in

                        the night

            driveway,mybrain
              Home...home...
Tommy, Mary, Kathy, Becky, Deirdre, Hope, Patrick, born
  with the woman
      I little knew truely   Mother, warmth, in
    the house, now, summer warm air & the lights
    of - the human   The Fallons on Linden St/Rumford town
              How, light light. Death
                        at,
              only one way out

                            a ME
                turn, in the night air,
              Bean Brook across
                      the street, noising

44

                                              dark ness...
                    let us
turning
(dog barking)

Turning. Into the night, my attention turns, with my body,
   to the walk to work, the high pitched whine
in the warm night air, the white-orange glow in the darkness
the paper mill, and I resist going to work
in that place
the horrifying sound, the violences against my self.
              Vibration of floors and tables, the pressure on my
mind and body.
              The speed of the machines, the savage environment.
the mill, to work. I hate the hate of the paper mill.   Horror
   The high-pitched whine the sound of the papermaking machinery.
Drive: straight. Drive, straight.   Lines.   Lines.
Jesus, I see Hope hitting the windshield of the car, thrown up
at into the windshield as the car spins, 3 girls bounced around
in the car I see, hitting the rear view mirror, snap off the
mirror Melissa Bryant breaking HER NOSE, 3 GIRLS WINDSHIELD
SPLINTERED BUT NOT BROKEN DENTED WITH HUMAN HEADS WITH HUMAN
HEADS GIRLS YOUNG HITTING THE WINDSHIELD AND BLOOD CUTS CAR
HITTING THE CONCRETE ABUTMENT AND STOPPED ON THE DARK ROAD THE
3 GIRLS SPUN AND HURT AND CRYING STUMBLING OUT OF THE BIG CAR
IN THEIR DRESSES BLEEDING AND CRYING HIT THE WINDSHIELD HUMAN
HEADS, GIRLS, STEERING WHEEL DASHBOARD FLOPPING AROUND IN THE
SPINNING CAR I SEE THEM HURT HURT HURT MY DAUGHTER HOPE HITTING
THE WINDSHIELD VIOLENCE, HER IMPOTENCE AGAINST DEATH, HUMAN
IN THE CAR VIOLENTLY SPUN AROUND ON THE HIGHWAY OUT OF CONTROL
AT RUMFORD CENTER, SPINNING BIG CAR, GIRLS, HATE I FEEL, I HEAR
I SEE THE HUMAN HEAD HITTING THE WINDSHIELD

6.

Soft dirt. Soft feet. Soft soul.
Soft soul.

Turning in the driveway, the dirt there not hard,
resisting, as the tarred sidewalk to the house, *the soft*
dirt, good, under my feet (shoed) feel the give in the dirt.

Warm air. Light, air, of the night, the summer.
Friendly air: light, warmth. No not: force of heat. Me,
surround, air lightened. Night. The darkness.

Orange-white glow in the air hated.

Foot moved, scraping the dirt, moving the dirt, softening.
Hatred: tar. Hard: noise. Noise. Against. This. Whine
(machines) night-darkness, beautiful air, eyes out! EYES OUT.

Softening sand under foot - boy. Child. *Hurt me.*
MOTHER I HAVE LOST YOU DADDY IS DEAD. I felt the night air,
looking in the darkness, to see the white orange glow in the
sky (over the town) from the lights of the paper mill.

I am an alien: I am not an alien.

Whining sound. Whining sound. whining Sound.

(Child, in begin: don't give. Take hard. return.)
I scraped my foot in the dirt, holding the basket over my
forearm. *And paper history book Dard Hunter -*

As we should resist...in self distortion.

To make. I will create, anew, as I feel the urge.
It's a necessity to free the "chained" spirit: *closed.* To
make alive, then, as before, free, my self, show, other human
beings, the hatred, violence, can be overcome - live.

Words: dirt, moving, under my feet. A softness,
delicacy, fulfillment through response from the dirt: the
language of the dirt - give, pass to others. A human foot in
a leather shoe, moving, feeling the scrape of shoe on dirt -
body sensing the whole movement into the dirt of the foot.

The words through the mind, moving in and out of
consciousness. Feel. Sense...the air. Hear the "sanding"
movement of shoe on dirt. Unresisting, dirt.

Touch, dirt...

I leaned over, to touch the dirt, feel in my fingers the
slight coolness, roughness, of the small place, I touched with
my fingers. A "sweetness", to my self, relinquishing its
essence to my self open to the dirt; dirt as dirt.

Open, self, to, air, summer, lightness.

Creation: my self, dirt. (I would. No! Don't go.
Fake, lie: cheat "Them". Holding at the in. FAKE!) Willow
on the lawn, the tree on the grass dark.

So between the trees we walked I did not want to go but
mother said yes go ahead we'll meet you at the fork in the
road the picnic

and she made me play softball in the tall grasses with
the other kids, child I wouldn't

we ate the picnic lunch together

on the mountainside

and when we were ready to go home the two families, the
mothers packed up the leftovers and lunches

encouraging us,
the oldest girl to go down the dirt road I'd never seen, boy,
and the fear in so I finally halfway down the road began to
cry and they asked why, she

for I wanted to go back to my mother because

I was lost and she couldn't meet me in that strange road
sided by bushes green taller

than the little boy five
crying

as I turned and ran, panicking
she ran after me
to catch me and she did catch me and held
me strongly, tugging I she talked to me for the road around
and bend bushes was the end
and my mother two mothers would be in the cars waiting for
all "no one else crying" Tommy cried

alone, scared to be alone
because he was lost and his mother wouldn't
be

able to find him. the big girl pulled him and he went

sniffling down the dirt road to see find his mother she sat
in the black Chevy car waiting motor and he climbed in
beside his brother to sit and drive away mother he knew the
fear, end as in the day light darkness came, to the child,
hard reality, change change first

aware of death of him self no one, he would not say death
to any, mother but
        the dirt under foot, Tom, here, natural. To create,
after facing death, little boy, there is no other challenge,
fear existing, to make, little one, self, in the face of death —
finality. close mind, from self — no mind: remake,
the beautiful, the love, the vitality, in earth, air,
transcend only so the end of life/self: change the world,
without fears, only one fear exists, one threat, little, as
free-floating
        boy walk between the library shelves, no not see the
card catalogue, wander to see if it exists here in the books,
somewhere, in a book to see the right words now to fit, the
fictions shelves, novels.
                        as walking, taking down a book
to read the blurbs and first words.
        return the book to the shelf if it did
   not fit the mind then, move on to read as the walking
boy eyes moving mind across book spines, then colors and
author's names the titles, in the quiet aisles of the library
shelter from the hot summer sunlight only the single light
bulbs shaded by opaque etched glass shades, a coolness and shade
alone to think
for the movement
                of eyes over the novel titles, writer's
names
freedom to wander aimlessly, to then
                think w/out authority, freely thought

                to wander boy, of quietness here
                    in the darkened aisles between
                        the library shelves dark

                                   wood stain
                                      comfort
                                         freed
                               the depth boy
        seeking a book to read or the art section painters
Michelangelo Rembrandt yes both and even the new ones
Cezanne van Gogh, but Rembrandt, the eyes - soul existing -
him self - and the sacrifice for art not the social status
but after the moving
        stopped I read *Men of Art*, Rembrandt the man. face fat
      human, in the dark, peculiar light
      from walking the aisle looking without
instruction
a book
         to learn as the mind would discover the
right ideas to see
                   from the random everyday search of the book
shelves Rumford dark stained wooden shelves of books
books words uncounted
                  no rule to find the word and ideas to
fit the boy's mind growing at 14 then Rembrandt art,
      the creation
                    Bean Brook running under the steady dull
ignoble whine in the summer air, paper mill, my thought
in the memory
      paper, for words: my words, to create. *urge, as*
necessity, yes. I know and will create: find from
            search
                  "Tommy! Tommy!"
            my little hand made
                        the letters on paper,
                  painted
                        trying hard
      to make the letter just right, and

                                    my mind
                                 preparing for
                           the work, creation, as
                           the discipline mom

to make the right
form of the letters, the letter
make the "germinal" mind
tough,
for the struggle
creation only, integrity
of the boy, "truth"
creation
until to remake
the form
a necessity - vitalize as
is the urge to create,
the source, near the source
to clarify
creation only is the
crux
not money
but a
form freeing my self
into the creation,
renew, child, the man, from
your creative
the source
fresh, fresh,
break

old forms

break down
the unnecessary,
recreate
recreate

a new form naturally
in
risk,
yes, so
it's "damn true" not

50

                                    an imitation
                    but the mind wandering in search
                                    of the creation
                                    of the creation
                            through itself with
                                    itself, in
                            freedom of itself

                            floating in itself,
                                    creation to
                be
                            looking, with the
                                    mind
                            as the self
                                    in chaos
                of the unconscious
    for the moment
            of "revelation", the new creation,

                being
                                    alone, defiant
                            of forms, behavior
                                    afraid, as
                                    always
                    to risk, the urgent risk to go on the
                    search
                            for the source, to catch
                            for a moment all in one
                                    creation
                    belief it could be done the only
        certainty that blind belief prior knowledge of
                                    reality
                            a knowledge there
                there inside
                        no one taught, safe
                    in this urgent self, seeking
        a connection conscious to the creation

                              freeing the unconscious
                          transferal of the
                                        true creative
                                                 energy
                                    the power of the self
                                            pressing
                    blindly any way
                    to find the power in the creation for the
                                         self existing
                                    Body urgent, cry
on this single planet
here, in the universe   for creation, for Creation
    I can know   seething
the whole creation,   after this "truth"
its source in my self   and communication
and in its self   in the chaos
one,   of creation
my experience, life on the planet,
in Rumford Maine   here, chaos
                                             seen,
                                  the necessary risk
                                  the agony of chaos
                                    of the self in
                                          the self

                                  body urging power

                              in the creation – creation
                                        to creation
                                    creation only,
physically
the boy, man in the driveway of dirt (Rumford) still is
on a delicate balance
                              a fine perfection, balance
                                       in the mind

child, child, child, child   insisting on "truth"
                                          on paper

the paper mill, making paper, the "sacred" material, alienating
with its violence, to the human, now, in the night, always in
    daylight: a horror, not imagined, for the soul. seeking
creation, paper made for money: not paper because it is a tool
for the human being to develop intellect, to seek the truth of
material and spiritual world, to seek "truth" - but, there,
paper, in the Rumford valley, there, on which lies written yes;
deceptions typed and xeroxed by the management, "manipulation"
of the incredible human mind, human beings, the soul - not for
beauty. not for love. not for justice (somewhere a human
being uses Rumford-made paper to fight for justice, yes, the
paper company shareholders, managers and millworkers, to lie,
yes depend on to live, the lie) *iron, speed* -
    so, the "Almighty Dollar" reigns supreme - almost, almost -
in this good old Rumford & the LIE -
corruption CORRUPTION
        of the word - THE LIE A REALITY,
                "shure, becuz we gotta eat"
                                                          &
                "you can't fight City Hall"
                        the lie, VISCIOUS   USE
USE/   of the word,   I am horrified by the lie..
          bald faced opportunists -
writers use, moneymakers use of the human word
their "murder" of the language, A CREATIVE USEFUL TOOL
                                        of beauty
"death" of the word, the "sacred word"
          and creativity,
                DEATH   of the human spiritual,
IMMORALITY
OF THE WORD
                    RAPE OF THE AESTHETIC "TRUTH"
                      of perfection
                      denial
                          of "the truth's"
                  necessity, art,
and human love, prostitution (& how I corrupt the word) yes
        so difficult to write....

unwittingly,

unwillingly, do we sometimes
PROSTITUTE the word, human integrity we should be watched the
self-righteous especially   WATCH THE RIGHTEOUS
                                    FOR HIS/HER CORRUPTION
OF   THE WORD ...)   the subtlety of human intellect
            the "beauty" of corruption, by the intellect of
                            the   SACRED WORD
- STILL, we must search out the "snopes" -
  pimping the word
pimping the world!
search out the "snopisms" IN OURSELVES / some of these guys
THE TRUTH IS TOUGH , HARD , HARSH
            some of these guys make the paper, the idiots!
(make paper, not beautiful to the senses - sense - no
  fulfillment of the sense - No, to the eye, and
not to the finger's touch: no sense, no beauty .)
                        writers, (creators) TOO
                                seek POWER, words; use
                                TO MANIPULATE
                        MINDS   personal
                        control/ "status"
in society, false, yes, ideas
for personal POWER over others   WITH-holding "truth", etc.
                            DO NOT   DO NOT
investigate   truth
                    (to live well
                    NOT risk art, self-
                    prostitution in
                        other words
                            Ezra, YEAH! -)
        TO EAT WELL - LIVE COMFORTABLY
yeah, & to speak "comfortably"
they write so very "comfortably" - unAmerican/crossing US 1st
Amendment   w/SELF CENSORSHIP.. FEARING isolation from the
GROUP, THE GROUP - fearing   RISK - THE RISK of self

in the creation..   FEARING OSTRACISM

from   THE GROUP

HEY! PAPER - TO TELL "TRUTH" ON! That's to fry their butts
fellah! Ha ha ha!

*it is a sin for a writer to prostitute the word the world in
    the dirt, my foot, soft dirt; human foot.* (to write
truely, honestly, of life, of my experience, the experience of
living, on this planet in the universe, as honestly as possible,
to learn, as much as possible, judging yourself, yes, my self,
as often as possible, not to lie, omit, not to distort, how can I
see the truth, write the truth) *human*...

I must go to work. 11-7. 3 shifts to work. 11-7, 3-11, 7-3.
Back to 11-7 again. Around the clock, from one shift to another:
11-7, 3-11, 7-3. The paper testing lab - used to be Quality
Control, now Product Services, paper tested before it leaves the
mill. Machine foreman will know if the paper can leave the mill
for a customer, the one he's making it for - should be transferred
to another customer, less fussy one, who has older, slower presses
machines - should be "beatered", recycled into the papermaking
system for another run on the paper machine because the paper's
no damn good. Christ, I hate to go to work. House lights a
light yellow, warm yellow, inviting me, I feel, night, invite
myself, back into the house, home, to .sleep. To sleep, night, as
I should, normal people do, should. (Many "abnormal" people in
Rumford - 11-7 tonight.) Dirt, scuff foot, Jackie in the house,
three kids still at home, asleep. I work. Walk, then, the dread
repressed, of the violent paper mill. The Lab quiet. 11-7.
"Graveyard shift". If I get a chance, I'll read the manuscript,
think it over, if I don't have time because the work load is
heavy, the paper machines running good, fast orders. Test paper.
I'm P-1 tonight. Check the strength of paper, Elmendorff Tear
machine, testing tearing strength in 2 directions - machine and
cross-direction. Opacity, opaqueness, with opacimeter; the
color, color subtleties of the white paper, red yellow and blue.

Mind in movement, the tear test, creation, in the mill, Rhonda,
Steve, Jerry, I, testing paper, work, living. Think next piece
to write, connected to one in my lunch basket, think, maybe write,
get some notes down, for next piece, make some corrections. Work.
Money. 8 hours. Over, over, same tests, for #2, 4, 5, 6, 7, 8,
9 paper machines, paper samples, for 8 hours. Make unconscious-
conscious work together: keep away from rule of conscious over the
unconscious, only go into unconscious often, often, test paper, 8
hours. High pitched whine, walk, then, white-orange glow in the
night sky dark, make money. Above all things, money. Yes, paper –
change the world somehow, go away from house, home, safety, lighted
yellow warmth in the night, bedroom, typewriter, books, writing-
create, go to the work in its realities, a part. Dirt, foot. To
use of words, tonight, talking, to the lie, to the truth, the whole.
Make money, Tom, tonight, in the paper mill: $10.93 an hour,
testing paper. Add 21 cents shift differential an hour, for the
11-7 shift – good money, I make in the paper mill, yes. Eat good.
Dress good. When all the kids are gone, I'll have more money'n
I can "shake a stick at" – get ready for retirement at 62. If I
live long enough. I'm doing OK. Not making beautiful paper,
making "machine-made" paper – making money. VIOLENCE.
                    walk creation away from that place in
the distance light color the building the light yellow
                                                color
            known in the daylight from the lawn
a mound in front of the house banking on the edge a willow
        in the dark dark shape and the house
                a two story
                frame vinyl siding known windows
                        lighted on the first story the living
room and the addition part visible from the dirt driveway
rectangular
    shaped house building on granite ledge
driveway cut out of the ledge rises to the house short the
                                        front walk tar and
            narrow leading to the house front door lighted
        warm yellow in the night forced front walk and the

small house next door left
   mother-in-law last year died
the yard behind both houses bushes and the swamp then behind
                                                        both
            houses
the garden reaching way to the hills spring, water filling
the swamp from melting snow off the hills at the end of
Holyoke Street the swamp the light colored house warmly
     lit, family and where writing creating a vital
  lives children some love and some fighting pain of
            marriage over 25 years not an easy for the security
still when creation necessary, the paper in the bedroom
   on the second story,
               front room words written, though in an
    ordinary
               place small town is Rumford and the Ford Escort
     beside me in
the driveway on my arm, lunch basket for the mill, paper
mill walk creation away from the house of human safety
   comfort to the paper mill then
on the street Spruce Street a car passing by the house
                              me headlights paper I know for
            human words that my place is home and the Lab and
     payday familiar life of a man on earth then is
walk
for the familiar house behind turning
warm lights warm lights yet I am
            warm, paper home Tom walking in the darkness yours
in the warm air and water noising from Bean Brook and the
               whine of the paper mill machinery in the familiar
         darkness of the town for the Shorey's are neighbors
      in the urgent work of creation, words, me, the
    lunch basket
so walk, the water of Bean Brook in my ears, the warm summer
            air, night, warmth
                  and the house, lighted   walk to work in
         the paper mill tonight, up Spruce Street
         the hill up Maine Avenue

dog barking, so slowly walk, then, turn away from home

I smiled, as I walked past Shorey's house, away from the
driveway, grandaughter Brandi in mind. Shorey's a nice place.
Twenty years in the mill today. Fred's retired just last
year, Beater Room Super from hourly, forty plus years in the
mill. And Arthur Arsenault, my other neighbor, retired,
hourly, a painter. June 22nd, (fifty years old), little
Brandi melts me...but a war, it was a "hell" with Mary her
mother growing up...tenacious "two beasts"...home, little Brandi,
born, and I was nervous...first birth for Mary...and, not in
our hospital...so that my mood changes to elation when I see
Brandi, the child in me alive. all anger...I bridled, raged,
against the marriage - she in high school seeing a kid graduated
kid a drinker...she'd wear faded dungarees to school...she says
"loose", my last word, or "place", Brandi always the last word...
Brandi walks on little human legs around the house from room
to room... the idiot waited too long for the baby to be born -
then decided on a caesarian, and Jackie in the labor room with
Becky...breathing, breathing to help Mary...Brandi, stands in
the den, eyes wide, lips pursed, puts an arm around Spice - the
little dog - bending from the waist, kisses him on the back...
no knowledge...brings a hairbrush out of the living room...it's
over, the shouting father...she went out with him..."Punkin, come
see Grampy"...so we went to MacDonald's and she was excited
standing in the den, fat in her turquoise jacket, white fur hat
and lavender boots, "Donald's, Donald's!", her eyes wide, alight,
innocent...and I would not back down, ever, I was right in what
I wanted for my daughter, but mother talked to Mary while I
raged aloud, "blew the roof off", mother supported Mary, allowing
her to go out with the kid..."Grampy! Grampy!"...so Jackie took
Brandi into the living room after lunch at MacDonald's to lay
down for her nap and she fidgeted, babbled, crawled all over
her Nanny, fell asleep finally on her grandmother's shoulder...
both asleep...innocence, light, so light the baby's breathing...
Brandi...Jackie asleep...

and a man walking
   a little boy from the beginning
   mind open, in time, to know and to be, alive

  :the opening up/splitting
  my mind
    & the unease
    pressure,
       begins
  as a darkness/*i see*
       mind
,a chaos
   i would not/cannot

  seek-
    it is a deep/

    wildness
      coming on
     coming on   fear
wildness, ,
     this hole;
    will never,
     pass

   because it exists/
   in
    universe.

          openeng,

7.

And standing on the street here - human feet on tar -
                              Spruce Street, across
    from Shorey's and my own home - houses alight -

  the "moon" round and huge in the sky, tonight
   the "moon" which we know because human beings have visited, and
      stood upon, walked, upon, left
        the planet, "earth", have, for the first time, ever,
     leaving the "earth", to walk on an alien other-earth object
in space,

   in the universe, in "our solar system", looked back to
      that place left, a "ball" in the space

of the universe from the "moon" - see creation, "earth"

        from that distance of the "moon", see
   "earth", and think
                     on a place in the universe
 where, inside the specially constructed suits without which human
    beings would quickly die, walking slowly
    and
          awkwardly, with so little gravity to hold the men to
  the "moon's" hard surface - that "moon", there, in the sky
  - space - (we were, for the first time

 [in] the universe - seeing creation, the blue and white
    colored planet there in space, our creation:
      our minds developed through language and writing
   - books - on paper now - human beings living so clearly
 in the universe, standing on the "moon", and,
                  we heard their voices, saw their movements
 relayed to "earth" from the "moon", to us, here,
                      in front of TV's in

living rooms, on "earth", saw
the human beings, walk on the "moon".
   that "moon", there, in the sky, above me, now, above
Tom Fallon, here

   in Rumford, above all human beings in town,
 moving, "moon" moving, in space, creation.
"Our moon", every day and night - the man on the "moon", now -
seen.   Space, seen, known, understood,

creation.   With the human mind...the "earth" is known

from the "moon",
 and I see the "moon" tonight, from the "earth", here, where I, on
feet   human being, was created, live. As I walk, here,
on "earth", (a planet in the Milky Way galaxy),
   life, to work the 11-7 shift in a paper-making mill:

A human, a creation, thinking, creating...THE "MOON" IN THE UNIVER

THERE   Walk. *Feet; human*... (I am walking to work
in the paper mill, because I want to make money.)No poetry.
The "moon" solid, no poetry.
(Human feet on tar, in Rumford, [earth]: human

feet , on the "moon", [in the universe].) Poetry?

                       For work, Tom.

                  [moone! there!]
                   "Mind", on the "moon"
there - here.   Such a distance, in the mind, and world,
 universe

        in mind . And, feet, in the softness of dirt, shoe,

PIECE II - SOUNDING

This afternoon.   Restless from typing *Piece I*, my mind,
I, began
to wander for other ideas to work out in TMOTM - I looked
thru my old newspaper column for
the Rumford *Times*, "Sounding" - some published
some not published

skimming them
but reading those which caught my interest then

                    Quietly, now.....thought.....
          a painter.....Francis Bacon.....
                              English.....

                         Modern aesthetic.....
                Quietly, now...thought.......

               to make the human figure.....
                       Paint, the human...

          from the human mind, create.....
          Bacon paints human beings.....

     on the canvas surface.....rectangles.....
           he, painted, human, beings.....

          Where do these beings come from...
               quietly, thought...now.....

Francis Bacon, his beings.....
Distorted shapes.....in the rectangles.....

the movement of form, human.....
shape changed, a distortion.....

in the silence of the rectangle..
...thought, in paint.....

Unhuman.....beings.....human, beings.....

Inside the rectangle.....beings.....
or, torn beings.....

not, simply, shapes.......
Distorted physical shapes.....

Thought. Quiet.
Deep, the beings, painted from...

From inside the human being's thought.....

From the quietness of human thought..
Form, angular.....ugly, form.......

Francis Bacon painting human beings...
Distorted.

human beings; shaped like agony.......
from within the Bacon human mind.....

Curse:

In the rectangle's quiet, a curse.....

painting, now, human beings, in horrible shapes.

Horror.

Thought.....horror....

are ugly thoughts painted on canvas..

Horror, of human life...behind glass.......

an artist paints the soul.....inside a

rectangle.....(today)..

Horror. Don't speak. Scream. And human.....

This was the kind of stuff Paul Gates let me publish in the one-horse town weekly, the Rumford *Times*.

I am disappointed that my kids are growing up.   I am because I am losing that innocence that is only in the very, very young - the very pure.

What brings this on now?

Bath night - Friday nights at the Fallon household.

When you have seven children, bath night can be quite a ritual.   It isn't a simple matter of getting in, washing down, rinsing off and getting out, and it's all over in a half hour - there is a pleasure that the little children get out of the bath that seems to add hours to the task.

When the kids were all young, I would sometimes go through the whole bunch, all seven, washing hair, washing pink and white dirty little faces and knees and feet, the kids happy as only kids can be to get into the tub and swish around in the soap suds.

Now I can only wash the two little ones - the older girls won't let me in the door now that they are eleven, twelve and thirteen - and the other night, Dee, who is now eight, wouldn't let me bathe her!

So, this Friday night, little Hope and Patrick stripped down and climbed into the bath water "spiked" with bubble bath. I watched them play in the water for a while - they weren't too active because Daddy was there, but they did have a good time - then I decided it was time to wash hair - (watch the eyes, Daddy, the shampoo hurts the kids' eyes, I admonished myself) as I very carefully soaped their hair and rinsed -

After Patrick's short hair, I had to soap him down and run the washcloth over his tiny little pink and white body - the body of a five year old in kindergarten - you should have seen the smile on his face - you could have lit a thousand suns with the radiance of his little face! And the dancing in his eyes must have been what brought life into existence in the first place - he was so very happy to get a bath, to be in the warm and white bubbly water - it made me very happy to be touching and soaping and finally drying the oh so perfect creation of this little boy - !

(Yes, this is Dad - pure, sentimental Dad! Sometimes, I would like to cry - yes, this is true - when I think that these beautiful little children will someday have to die. I don't want them to die for they are the essence of human beauty, they are the most perfect and loving beings in a man and a woman's life - this is why a man and a woman are married, and why they share their life and love together, for it is only their own happiness that brings the creation of new life, these so perfect and happy little human beings.

I am not going to apologize for bringing ordinary human sentimentality into the newspaper, for it seems to be an important and very good, part of human life.)

Well, after Patrick it was Hope's turn to be washed - with her long hair and her oh so chubby little body. The shampoo was Jasmine scented and she asked me what color the flower was and I told her, then she picked up some soap suds from the water and told me of the very purest flowers - oh yes, she

*actually did - there were flowers in the soap suds of the
bathtub for her - and happiness for me.*

*Well, the Friday night bath ritual is over - I climbed
in after the kids for my bath too - and we're all lying on
Mom and Dad's bed - all seven plus two - watching television -
this is the family that can exist on earth in moments of simple
happiness, these are the human moments to remember.*

*Yes, someday I will remember the Friday night bath ritual
at our house and I will be sad - for I will have lost the so
perfect innocence and beauty that I had with my children in
a bathtub - yes, Dad will miss Friday nights with the whole
family of little children - they will be gone forever.*

As you can see, I changed the temper of the "Sounding"
articles from week to week.

Let's face a fact of life: I can be as phony as anyone
else in Rumford.

Remember the lead article of "Sounding" when I told you
that my writing was going to be a real benefit to readers of
this newspaper?

What a pretentious phony!

Someone should have shouted at me for that pretentious
article - yes, I said that I was going to do something for
you that others could not do because my ideas were different
and vital - aside from the fact I'm getting paid for writing
my own little newspaper column - a status point!

FALLONEY BALONEY!

That's what they call me in the Quality Control Lab
sometimes - "Falloney Baloney, full of pizza pie and macaroni!"
And then they laugh at me! It's a little joke to keep my head
on earth - to keep my head the "right size" - !

Now who am I really kidding? Am I doing something wonderful
for people in Rumford by writing this little newspaper column?

Let me tell you how this phony business started.

Last week I read in this newspaper about the increased circulation at the Rumford Public Library - and right away I thought to myself, *Who are you kidding? What the hell good is increased circulation at the library if good books aren't being read?*

Then I thought spontaneously - *Well, what are you doing for the town with this little two-bit article of yours that makes you qualified to criticize people obviously involved in serious, and good, work for the community?*

I wasn't sure I liked that question, but it jumped into my mind anyway - I was stuck with it.

And, yes, I called myself a phony -

Who am I to say that people aren't reading good books right along with all the fiction that is just sappy entertainment? (I hadn't even asked what people were reading!)

I jumped to conclusions! Like the little snob I can be sometimes - an irritating little snob always promoting the "Fine Arhts" and "Fine Lit'rachoor".

I mean let's face it, the "Fine Arhts" and this "Fine Lit'rachoor" haven't solved the world's problems in this century or in any other for that matter - in fact, no amount of good literature - "Fine Lit'rachoor" - has stopped humankind from waging war, has it?

Well, I had to back off a little bit - I mean, I couldn't very well say that all that sappy entertaining fiction was less beneficial to people here in Rumford than Little Tommy Fallon's "Fine Lit'rachoor", could I? (Not in print I couldn't!)

So it is I must ask you to give me the old horse laff when I get too big for my britches! When I become a little too self-righteous with my solutions to community and world problems, be sure you pick me up on it and holler loudly so I can hear you - "Hey, Falloney Baloney, you're full of pizza pie and macaroni, you know that!"

Remember - and I'm not kidding you now - the writer of this little two-bit article can be as pretentious, as PHONY, as anyone else in society - so watch me closely, watch me closely...!

Type is cold. Feel it —
There is a feeling to it. It's
mechanical.

This handwriting is surrounded
by type, of letters.
Look at it —

A handwritten word, is natural.
Hand writing flows.

Type, print, is hard. Severe,
in line, form.
Can you feel this severity in the
type on the pages here?

The natural grace, in the hand
writing? Naturalness.
Feel it — a yes.

"Awright, what kinda car you want? Somepin cheap, yeah,"
Hot Dog said.

"Yeah, somepin cheap," Dizzy echoed.

"They don't make no cheap cars no more, Dizzy, you know
that. It'll cost you an arm an a leg to keep anything in gas -
then you'll have to have it special fitted cuz you can't drive
it with one arm an one leg - that'll cost you more dough - you
ain't gonna get a cheap car nowadays, Dizzy, let's face it!

"No, no, Hot Dog - I wanta cheap car and I know that if
they don't make em yet they gonna make em cuz that car salesman
down at Tootie's tole me they make em real cheap nowadays!

"That's the kinda cheap y'mean," Hot Dog said.

"No. Now, lissen to wot this salesman tole me bout them
new cars - he sez they alredy make disposable fenders..."

"C'mon, Dizzy, he wuz pullin your leg!

"No, no, he wuz real serious! Now lissen to me Hot Dog!
I figgered if they makin cheap cars alredy, why can't they go
all the way an make the real thing?

"Waddya mean, the real thing?

"Lissen, Hot Dog - an don't tell nobody cuz we're gonna
make a billion on this one - lissen now - disposable diapers,
disposable pens, disposable razors, disposable clothes even -
get the idea?

"Hunh - no!

"Disposable cars! Get it? Disposable cars - jus like
them disposable diapers - they'll sell like hotcakes in this
country, Hot Dog!

"You mean you throw em away after so many miles? You're
a nut, Dizzy!

"Hey, wuz Edison a nut? Wuz Ford a nut? Nosirree, I ain't
no nut, Hot Dog, but everybody else is an I'm gonna capitalize
on it an make a mint!

"Nobody'll buy that idea, Dizzy.

"Oh yeah? I say that with everthing goin up like it is
we might jus as well buy disposable cars an throw em away afta
so many miles.

"Disposable cars, disposable cars," Hot Dog thought aloud.

"Yeah! The dream of the Great American Middle Class, the
future outta Detroit - disposable cars! An lissen, no one gets
killed in these new disposable jobbies becuz they gonna be made
a paper! People only get paper cuts - no one gets killed, right?
It's a real winner, I'm tellin ya Hot Dog!
    "Yeah...yeah....you're right, Dizzy. That's the real thing -
innovation - that's it Dizzy! That's the real thing!
    "Now you're talkin, Hot Dog! We're gonna make a mint!
Lissen to this for real innovation - 'No Deposit, No Return,
a Hundred Mile Guarantee an you can burn em in your own backyard'!
that's real American ingenewity - the whole country'll go crazy -
they'll all go crazy for Dizzy an Hot Dog's Disposable Cars!"
    So Dizzy and Hot Dog walk off into the American sunset with
their No Deposit, No Return, 100 Mile Guaranteed paper automobiles -
Dizzy Smith and Hot Dog Jones - the newest members of the American
Industrial Complex, the newest members of Billionaires Anonymous -
America Hurrah - America Hurrah!!!

    Paul Gates was my first editor at the little Rumford weekly
newspaper when I began "Sounding" - he was straight from school -
when Howard James first bought the newspaper from Rowbotham. No
one knew what they were doing at first and they were willing to
experiment a little - that's why I was hired.
    I had a free hand with the column until James began to go
conservative - yeah, he joined the business community and he made
his social connections - it was only a matter of time before my
"different" focus irritated people much attached to the "Sacred
American Cows" and began to complain to James - Gates liked my
stuff because he was young and alive, so he protected me as long
as he could - then he left before he was completely committed to
"the system" - he got free!
    And they slid Tommy out the door - but we put the screws to
"the system" until guilt raised its ugly little head - we made
the American middle class in Rumford uncomfortable for a little
while - ha ha ha!

unappealing

an iron
culvert, water
flowing
      the narrow
      brook
      water run

under
alders leaning,
leafless
and
      leaves
      on the bank
      wet
along the bank the
dark leaves brown-
black
      simply, the dark
      moss wet moss
      of bank,
      leaves
water
water
      flow from culvert

and
the rotting tree trunk
fallen,
      barkless

sky, grey, cloud
the
water flows, flowing

running
from the iron culvert

the brook at roadside
unappealing. (bean brook)

The most significant appeal of Maine is its insignificant
quality. This is not to be advertised; it is to be ignored.

The wood yard and the wood room.
Of the paper mill.
Pulp truck: loaded with wood.
Beautiful?
Wood unloaded by the cranes in the wood yard. Swinging
chain-wrapped logs off the pulp trucks flatbed, up onto
the pyramidal shaped pile of logs.
Is the movement beautiful?
Visual beauty - the empty pulp truck?
The crane, at rest, a thing of beauty?
A machine of some aesthetic perfection?
The wood yard, with 3 cranes, 4 pulp trucks, crane motors
running, under the pale blue sky, a few cirro-cumulus clouds
high above.
Is this beautiful? - the metal wood room building,
rectangular, grey-painted, behind the pyramidal wood piles.
The crane motors running - is that sound beautiful?
Familiar.
As is the sound of the pulp trucks moving out of the
wood yard, motors idling, dark exhaust in the air, blue sky.
A sound not unfamiliar - not heard.
Pulp trucks, a part of our life, necessary to the
movement of the logs from the woods to the wood yard, the
paper mill.
Pulp trucks, (their) form, necessary, the black crane
boom, engine housing and caterpillar tracks, necessary. Money.

To make money for people: paper, to be sold for money.
The sound of motors, pulp trucks and cranes, idling in the
afternoon sun. This is necessity.

But is the sound of the idling motor a beautiful sound
for human ears?

(Not music - sound based on aesthetics, intellectual
form -)

Plunking sound of logs falling on other logs in the wood
pile, dropped by the crane.

Beautiful sound?

(Is it a natural sound?)

A necessary sound: logs plunking against each other in
the wood yard of a paper mill.

On a beautiful summer afternoon.

Yes.

What's the aesthetic value of the crane's motor, the pulp
truck's motor?

Ugly?

Is it an ugly sound to the human ear?

Not loud - from the bridge over the railroad tracks -
still, ugly, as sound?

In the wood yard - next to the crane and pulp truck, motors
idling - louder. The motors sounding near the human being's
ears.

The crane operator - truck driver.

Ears hearing the sound.

Ugly? This loudness?

Is the pulp truck ugly?

Is the crane ugly?

Look - at.

What do you see?

What do you hear?

In the wood yard of the paper mill?

What is beautiful? What, there, in the wood yard, fulfills
the necessity of the human soul, for the aesthetic?

What's ugly?
What's obscene...?
Listen to the crane and pulp truck motor...!

LET THE CRANE MOTOR AND THE PULP TRUCK MOTOR SOUND, THE
FORM OF THE CRANE AND THE PULP TRUCK, INTO YOUR SOUL.....

I put
        the "Sounding" articles back into the manila envelope
and into the desk drawer again
when I was through with them..

                                    I simply wanted
                                to let my mind rove
freely over
    something
not related to THE MAN ON THE MOON to explore any idea
    I had not yet accepted
as necessary

                        for TMOTM -
the freedom of my mind wandering

                        at "loose ends"
with
no goal, no necessary goal, simply moving, alive, looking
for a life   in an idea,   looking for a "live" idea

            in my mind, to be drawn out
                        by reading through
        the needless "Sounding" articles..
search,
search,
I encouraged my mind, go freely into the creation - live in
                                the world where
                you know nothing, live in your ignorance,
                        live in your life-vitality
    - my goal to destroy poetry, begin to create a new literary
form, useful

74

to our age, our thought, spirit -

    to revolt   against   the old forms and
throught patterns, replace the conditioned-reflex
                       of traditional
  thought, to be creative -
destroy and create - to make
  charteng
       a reality -
a new world-thought from the unconscious that has been coming
since the beginning of the century - create - get my mind
down to the wild place, let it go where freedom rules, no rules
exist, no form exists, chaos in my mind before form - A PRIORI
 - where destruction is - origins of life in the mind - original
mind-life - where the fury is - down into the mind - search
into creation - read something unrelated to my goal, read
senselessly, trying to find creation - after I had skimmed and
read through articles I didn't want to intrude on THE MAN ON
THE MOON, I put them back into the envelope and into the
drawer. I forgot them - I got the senselessness out
of the way   I need the arbitrary. I need to be arbitrary,

"sweetheart", [I hate The System. I LOVE THE REVOLUTION.

    I love Creation. (There is something in me
     wild & dangerous to The System.)
       I LOVE Creation...!]

I love The natural CREATION

PIECE III

1.

  And, the trees, grow. Trees, grow. Trees growing.
The brook flowing through the trees.
  And, trees, grow. Trees, grew. The trees growing.
The brook flowed through the trees.
  So that on the earth, land, in the earth.
The brook flowing through the trees.
  Tree. From the earth as is usual: a growth.
The brook flowed through the trees.
  Up from out of the earth the trees growing.
The brook flowing through the trees.
  Now the trees growing (in a forest) together.
The brook flowed through the trees.
  As alive. Trees, grow. Out of dirt, and, up.
The brook flowing through the trees.
  Into the air the trees were growing now.
The brook flowing through the trees.
  Tree. One tree. Small tree. Many small trees.
The brook flowed through the trees.
  Their smallness of size part of their treeness.
The brook flowed through the trees.
  Their smallness of size part of their treeness.
The brook flowing through the trees.
  And tall, tall trees also in the Maine forest.
The brook flowed through the trees.
  Pines. Hemlock; spruce; poplar. Also other trees.
Pines. Hemlock; spruce; poplar. Also other trees.
  The brook flowing through the trees.
So that we know the tree is beautiful.
  The brook flowed through the trees.
So that we know the tree is beautiful.
  The brook flowed through the trees.
So that, we know the trees are beautiful.
  The brook flowing through the trees.
Trees, then, existing as before history written.
  The brook flowed through the trees.
New growing as before in history the trees.
  The brook flowed through the trees.
Trees, then, existing as before in history.
  The brook flowing through the trees.
Millions of the growing trees from the earth.
  The brook flowed through the trees.
Now.
  The brook flowed through the trees.
Earth: land - dirt. This, and so, trees.
  The brook flowing through the trees.

But not our trees except they are the trees.
    The brook flowed through the trees with a little noise.
One tree is not only one tree but the tree.
    The brook flowing through the trees with a little noise.
Tree growing. Tree growing. Tree growing.
    The brook flowed through the trees with a little noise.
Trees' growth. Trees'growth. Trees' growth.

Trees' growth. Trees' growth. Trees' growth.

So the tree grows, grows, grows, as is usual.

The tree grows in the forest until it stops growth.

All trees grow. And many trees growing together.

Many trees growing become together a forest.

And, in the silence, under the growing trees.

Coolness in the shadowy silence of the trees.
Coolness in the shadowy silence of the trees.

Pines. Hemlock. Spruce. Fir. Poplar. Etcetera.

So that we, human beings, know beautiful trees.

So that we, human beings, know beautiful trees.

And the beauty in the shadowy silence under trees.

The tree is beautiful as the tree is beautiful.

You and I know that the tree is very beautiful.

The tree is not simply pretty to us. Not, then,

only a tree. It is a tree and also beautiful.

No. Now, the tree is beautiful. It isn't pretty.
No. Now, the trees are beautiful. They are not pretty.

Under the pines, in the grove, there is a coolness.

So that we walked in the forest under the pines there.
So that we walked quietly in the forest under the pines.

So that coming into a field without the trees.
The sun shining. The field with wildflowers.

Under the pines, in the grove, there is coolness.

No shadows from the trees in the field now.

One white pine half way across the field.

Queen Anne's Lace in the field - and the white pine.

Under the pines, in the grove, there is coolness.

A field, then, surrounded by trees, a forest.

The ever green trees, the forest, the field, the pine.

A field of grass with Queen Anne's Lace.

Flowers, field, trees - grass and the grass.

Under the pines, in the grove, there is coolness.
Under the pines, in the grove, there is coolness.

So, the grown flowers in the field with the grass.

Field, open to the sun's light; grasses, fading color.

Under the pines, in the grove, there is coolness.

No longer green, the grass. The grass grass still.
Field field. And, the flowers Queen Anne's Lace.

Sun the sun, the sun the sun the sun the sun.

Surrounded by the trees: dark needles, green.

Not, green grass now. Although greened trees.

As usual. The way the sun shines openly.

Without shadows: heat. No trees' shade.

No coolness in the field, away from the trees.

Under the pines, in the grove, there is coolness.

And, without the trees, a different beauty, in the sun.

Although the light and shade of the trees,

make a beauty, a changing beauty, exist.

There is the beauty of the trees in themselves.

As well, the needles around the trees, on the earth, copper.

Softness of the pine needles on the earth.

A soft, feeling, the needles, on the trees, too.

To sit on the fallen pine needles to rest.

Lay back. Lying, then, on the softness there.
Under the pines, in the grove, there is a coolness.

Lay back. Lying, then, on the softness there.

To lay, and, to rest, as it is a necessity now.

Under the pines with the softness of green pine needles.

Eye: rested. Mind. Now, the green, in that coolness

of the pine grove. Copper pine needles on the earth.

Shadows from the trees.
Shadows from the trees.
Shadows from the trees.
Shadows from the trees.

And also I see the patterns: light and shade.
Trees. Tall tall trees around my body now.
Trees. Tall tall trees around my body now.

Away from the field with its harsh sunlight.

The direct sunlight from the sun in the grass field.
The direct sunlight from the sun in the grass field.

(A different kind of thing is this sun shining direct.)

The trees alive now.

The restness grows now in this body here.
The trees, forest, pass the rest to me.

Rest.
Rest.

Rest. In the coolness, from, that coolness.

Under the trees: rest's growth. Growing.

A body, my human body, growing with rest.
Resting in the shadows of the tree, the trees.

On the earth, soft the pine needles copper color.

Body; body: rest. Rests. Resting. This rest.
Perfect.

Under the trees, the restfulness, in the mind, too.
Under the trees, the restfulness, in the mind, too.
Under the trees, the restfulness, in the mind, too.

Trees. And, the growth. As then the beauty, too.
A perfection in the shadows of the pine trees, the trees.

Yes, I'll admit that the living trees die.
Yes, I'll admit that the living trees are dying.

Although, dead, the trees, express a beauty.

In the forest. The fallen trees are too beautiful.

The fallen, the dead, trees, are rotting.
            The fallen, the dead, trees, are rotting.
The wood, bark, rotting, and so crumbling.
            The wood, bark, rotting, and so crumbling.
Bark, rotting from the fallen tree. Bark, a death.
        Bark, rotting from the fallen tree. Bark, a death.
Tree dead or dying in the forest of the trees.
        Tree dead or dying in the forest of the trees.
Trees all around the fallen tree: fallen leaves.
        Trees all around the fallen tree: fallen leaves.
The leaves had fallen from the trees to the earth.
        The leaves had fallen from the trees to the earth.
And, now, the leaves, matted together under trees.
        And, now, the leaves, matted together under trees.
The cool air. Rotted tree. Rotted trees. Branches.
        The cool air. Rotted tree. Rotted trees. Branches.
Leaves and fallen trees among the living.
            Leaves and fallen trees among the living.
The trees standing upright in the cool air.
            The trees standing upright in the cool air.
Sun patterns on the fallen brown leaves here.
            Sun patterns on the fallen brown leaves here.
A beauty - human recognition - of dying.
            A beauty - human recognition - of dying.
And the strong living trees, the fresh cool air.
        And the strong living trees, the fresh cool air.
Dead. Trees. Rotting. Branches are rotten.
        Dead. Trees. Rotting. Branches are rotten.
Dead and dry. Moss covered. Dry branches.
        Dead and dry. Moss covered. Dry branches.
In the forests, with the dead leaves, rotting.
        In the forests, with the dead leaves, rotting.
In the forests, with the dead leaves, rotting.

                    In the forests, with the dead leaves, rotting.
Beautiful.
                                                        Beautiful.
Negative, it is, the human being thought alone.
                Negative, it is, the human being thought alone.
Yes, negative, the dead tree, yet, with a beauty...
                Yes, negative, the dead tree, yet, with a beauty...
Yes, negative, the dead tree, yet, with a beauty...
                    Trees. One tree. Treeness. And, living.
Air. In its coolness: freshness. And the trees.
                    Trees. One tree. Treeness. And, living.
I, feel, the affinity, with these trees.
                    I, feel, the affinity, with these trees.
Lying on my back among the pine trees.
                    Lying on my back among the pine trees.
I, a human being, know, in my way, trees.
                    I, a human being, know, in my way, trees.
As I know trees; that is, am one with the trees.
                    As I know trees; that is, am one with the trees.
Communion with these trees here lying on my back.
                    Communion with trees here lying on my back.
Lying on the earth, pine needles, on my back.
                    Lying on the earth, pine needles, on my back.
Tree. Tree. Trees. Tree. Trees. Trees. Tree.

Winter: I think, of snow, remember, trees.   In the forest,
        the dark green pines, white snow.
And, again, again, the, a beauty, with trees.   And, again,
        again, the, a beauty, with trees.
White. Whiteness. Of snow. Snow and pines.   White snow
        under the dark green pine trees.
Branches of dark green, with the white snow.   Branches of
        dark green, with the white snow.
The white snow on the pine tree's branches.   Cold, snow.
        Cold air. Yet, the air fresh.
A substance the air, cold, in the pine forest.   A substance
        the air, cold, in the pine forest.
With the white snow. White snow falling.   Over all the
        trees, and to the earth below.
Fall: snow. Quietly, falling, the whiteness.   Fall: snow.
        Quietly, falling, the whiteness.
Around the trees the white snow fell. Snow.   Snow. Trees.
Treeness. (This human being can know directly.)   Treeness.
(This human being can know directly.)

Feel, the treeness, in the forest. Feel trees. The woods
    on the hills, walking through trees.
The woods on the hills, walking through trees. Alone, to
walk, through trees, and, so, to think. Snow.
TREE   only, trees.   HERE   everywhere, growing.
The creation. The trees around me...   The creation.
    The trees around, me...

And, the trees, grow. Trees, grew. Trees growing.
                        The brook flowing

through the trees.
AND, THE TREES, GROW. TREES, GREW. TREES GROWING.
                        The brook flowing

through the trees.
And, trees, grow. Trees grew. The trees growing.
                        The brook flowing

through the trees.
AND, TREES, GROW. TREES GREW. THE TREES GROWING.
                        The brook flowing

through the trees.
So that on the earth, land, in the earth. Earth.
                        The brook flowing

through the trees.
SO THAT ON THE EARTH, LAND, IN THE EARTH. EARTH.
                        The brook flowing

through the trees.
Tree. From the earth as is usual: the growth.
                        The brook flowing

through the trees.

TREE. FROM THE EARTH AS IS USUAL: A GROWTH.

                              THE BROOK FLOWING

THROUGH THE TREES.

UP FROM OUT OF THE EARTH THE TREES ARE GROWING.

                              THE BROOK FLOWING

THROUGH THE TREES.

NOW THE TREES ARE GROWING (IN A FOREST) ALL TOGETHER.

THE BROOK FLOWING THROUGH THE TREES.

                              Now the trees

growing (in a forest) all together.

                              THE BROOK FLOWING

THROUGH THE TREES.

NOW THE TREES GROWING (IN A FOREST) ALL TOGETHER.

                              Armstrong stepped down

to the moon's surface.

So that on the earth, land, in the earth, it's so.

                              The brook flowing

through the forest.

Tree. One tree. Small tree. Many small trees. Yes.

                              THE BROOK FLOWING

THROUGH THE FOREST.

AND TALL, TALL TREES ALSO EXIST IN THE MAINE FORESTS.

                              Armstrong stepped down

to the moon's surface.

PINES. HEMLOCK; SPRUCE; POPLAR. ALSO THE OTHER TREES.

                              ARMSTRONG STEPPED DOWN

TO THE MOON'S SURFACE.

ARMSTRONG STEPPED DOWN TO THE MOON'S SURFACE.

THE BROOK FLOWING
THROUGH THE FOREST.   THE BROOK FLOWING THROUGH THE
FOREST.

The trees are growing on the hills behind our house.

Sex.
The trees are growing on the hills behind our house.

Love.
The trees are growing on the hills behind our house.

Human.
The trees are growing on the hills behind our house.

Paper.
The trees are growing on the hills behind our house.

The sky is sometimes a very light blue.
The trees are growing on the hills behind our house.

```
TREES
TREES
TREES
TREES
TREES
TREES
TREES
TREES
TREES
TREES
TREES
TREES
TREES
TREES
TREES
TREES
TREES spruce budworm moths
TREES spruce budworm moths
TREES
TREES spruce budworm moths
TREES spruce budworm moths
TREES
TREEE spruce budworm moths
TREEE spruce budworm moths
TREEE
TREEE spruce budworm moths
TREEE spruce budworm moths
TREEE
TREEE spruce budworm moths
TREEE spruce budworm moths
TREEE
TREEE acid rain
TREEE acid rain
TREEE acid rain
TREEE
TREEE acid rain
TREEE acid rain
```

85

TREEE acid rain
TREEE
TREEE acid rain
TREEE acid rain
TREEE acid rain
TREEE
TREEE acid rain
TREEE acid rain
TREEE acid rain
TREEE
TREEE acid rain
TREEE acid rain
TREEE acid rain
TREEE acid rain
TREEE clear cut
TREEE
TREEE clear cut
TREEE clear cut
TREEE clear cut
TREEE clear cut
TREEE
TREEE clear cut
TREEE clear cut
TREEE
TREEE clear cut
TREEE
TREEE clear cut
TREEE
TREEE clear cut
TREEE
TREEE clear cut
TREEE
TREEE clear cut
TREEE
TREEE clear cut
TREEE
TREEE
TREEE clear cut

```
        TREE
TREE
        TREE    cleaar cut
TREE            cleaar cut
        TREE    spruce budworm moths
TREE        spruce budworm moths
        TREE    spruce budworm moths
TREE        acid rain
        TREE
TREE            clear cut, acid rain
        TREE
tree        spruce budworm mothes
        TREE    cleaar cut
TREE
        tree
            acid rane, cleaar cut
tree
            acid rane,
        TREE
            cleaar cut, spruce budworm mothes, acid rane
tree
tree        acid rane, acid rane
tree
tree
tree            spruce budworm mothes, cleaar cut
trees           acid rane
```

```
                    I had to break
"the system" - I just had to - so I threw
this in - I had the feeling
                        that something had to be done
to break
            with the form I was developing in my mind as
I went along, so while I was looking for the section I'd already
written
about the raw material of paper - wood, trees - I happened

on this.  Concerning the raw material, but

                            put aside, saved
        for a reason I couldn't remember:  not what I was
looking
```

for.   Not the form I was looking for
in reality.

I used it, to break the "hard form" I felt solidifying
in my mind.

And, then, I used the section I'd been hunting for in the room,

which I eventually found in the file cabinet, one

of the file cabinets in the other room, next.
          Where it could rationally belong without upsetting
              the evolution of THE MAN ON THE MOON -
                  Break   break   break,   form....
                              (in. my. mind..)
          break into consciousness, rule..
to see what exists,   in reality

2.

Dog died in space.
American satellite
orbits Earth explore
Van Allen Belt natur
Explorer 1 orbiting.

Sputnik 1, 184 lb
Russian satellite
rocketed into orbit
around planet Earth.

1120 lb satellite
Sputnik 2 into space
with live dog inside.
Dog died in orbit.

Vostok 1 Russian spacecraft
orbited once around planet
Earth with man Yuri Gagarin.

Alan Shepard flew less
than one orbit around
Earth in U.S. Freedom 7.

Gemini 6 and Gemini 7 make a rendezvous in space of Milky Way galaxy.

Russian space capsule Voskhod 2 with Alexi Leonov for first walk in space around Earth.

Vladimir Komarov killed when Soyuz plummeted to the planet Earth.

Virgil Grissom Robert Chaffee
Edward White killed in space
capsule fire before leaving
planet Earth for the Moon.

Apollo 11 rocketed into
Milky Way lands module
on Moon. Neil Armstrong
walks on Moon and speaks
to people back on Earth.

92

Pioneer 10 flew
outside the solar
system 2.81 billi‹
miles from the Su›

Planet Earth orbits Sun.
And the Moon orbits the
Earth.   In the Milky Way
galaxy the dog died.

Reentry of Russian
spacecraft Soyuz 11
faulty seal, pressure
decrease killing
Dobrovolsky, Volkov
and Patsayev.

2 b.

The tall, thin trees at the side of the road were
rough-barked.

*Almost certain that I like this, although I wasn't
taught to...*

The dark green pine stand, the
softness-look of the pine needles.

I see the darkness in the pines;
a threat, I feel, in this darkness...

The leaves, broad, green, on the
small oak tree at the top of the
cut-away slope; the slope, a fine,
tan sand.

Railroad tracks. Boxcars.
Beside the tracks, rails
stacked, dark-rusted.

Wildflowers along the railroad
tracks. Light blue, small asters –

*I sat in the short grasses, tired
after work. I rested in the sun
before continuing on my way home.*

A line of boxcars on the tracks.
Two tank cars for chemicals. The
boxcars were old and dark.

*I lay myself back in the grass.
The sky was light blue with only
one white cloud moving. I felt
contentment in myself here.*

98

Cars and trucks pass on
the highway above the
railroad tracks.

I had a thought to write...
"wildflowers beside the road"
I wrote on the wrinkled paper,
and I continued to write...

Down the tracks, the wood
yard. Tracks lead under the
bridge to the Kraft Mill
where the chemicals break
down the wood chips into
pulp for the paper machines.

2 c.

The boy in the canoe bow,
dipping the paddle into the
lake water

In the open tent,

The tent sides were rolled
up. The four boys were sleeping
on iron cots, the sun rays

The pines were high above the tents of
the camping site.

The trees were white pines

He usually took a canoe out on
the river. The lily pads - turtles
in the shallow water - the river passed
between Panther Pond and another pond

In the woods, the fields, along the
dirt road, along the pine needled paths,
around the pine trees' roots protruding
from the earth

Trees are cut down
with a chainsaw

    Trees, marked by a forester;
    these are the only trees cut

    The tree is felled by a single man
    and then cut into four foot lengths,
    is loaded on a truck

Boise Cascade land is selectively
thinned, leaving trees to grow
larger for future cutting

    Single, big treed trunks, limbs
    cut, are dragged by horses or
    oxen to a clearing for

        Mechanical skidders drag
        many tree trunks to a
        clearing
Chipped in the clearing, the chips
are blown into a van – or sized
to four foot lengths – or as long
logs – transported to the paper
mill

The chainsaw makes a harsh noise in the woods

  muddy, deeply rutted logging roads

        Independent loggers, alone, in
        winter snow, chewing tobacco

2 d.

alone, in the chair

to think about life...

not understanding life as other
people understand

always in the back of his mind,
death, and this knowledge,
making him question

alone:

that end of life, to stop
his consciousness of life,

eyes no longer see;
eyes no longer

no brain to think:
death. the grave

102

my only defense, my thought...

to know,   or

to be,

does   the soul   exist

2 e.

        to   thin

    the 30   acres of
                    red pine
        in Gilead
                        Maine

                        thin,
        thirty acres
                        of red pine
        at Gilead:

                        to cut trees

        so others
        maintain   their growth
                        rate

                        for future

        harvest –

104

                          thin
                     red pine
        in Gilead,
            cutting   trees so other
                           trees

            could gain

                             space for
               growth

                             &, to experiment
        with whole tree

                             chipping in the
                             woods
           :mechanized

                             w/new machines
                             & fast –

               to thin   30 acres of red
                              pine

at Gilead
    so remaining   pines would gain
        space   needed for optimum

        growth:
      to use   whole tree chipping
                    in the woods

for the 1st time,
      mechanized   harvesting – the pines

      sheared   off
near the ground   & placed by the shear
                    machine with

other cut trees,
     the bunch   gathered by a skidder
                   & dragged to a clearing
       to be
                   chipped: the whole tree
                   chipped

    blown into
      a van   trucked to the mill
   : 3 days   thinning 30 acres

cut, use

to use as biomass :   to thin a 30 acre

tract of red pine   , burn
                                                for energy
the Gilead plantation
cut in 1978 (thinned)   planted in 1958, 7.5 ft
                                       by 7.5 ft spacing
(Boise forestry research)   & not to thin, give
                                       the pines room
to grow

1 diameter inch
every 3 years   harvest the trees

                                       "whole chip"
mechanize

   harvesting   pines sheared near

                                       the ground –
   only stumps –

                                       placed, then

by the Hydroax Shear

                                       w/other trees in a

                                       bunch

to be grappled by   the John Deere grapple
skidder, dragged
to a landing   *whole tree - whole,*

                             bank, twigs needles
- *chipped*

the whole tree   & blown into vans
                             trucked from Gilead
to the mill
- Morbark chipper -
                             1178 tons of biomass
harvested with little
damage
        to the other   red pines - *free space,*
then,
for these to grow in   : 4 to 10 years
                             another thinning operation
                             before the final
harvest
        of trees
    for use as pulp   to make paper in Rumford -

        thin   *trees*

Cut.

2 f.

&, at 48 years of age,

I have

actually

aged

in the morning

        I   am tired   :   I cannot rest
to
    return my energy

                        for working even
            easily
                in the small garden

    I   have   a   new & vital

                    meaning   holding   me

in the afternoon, sun
shining, hot

      summer day, after
8 hours at work in the mill
        2 days' work

I   feel   a   buoyancy

       in myself

or

   to think   -   I cannot write   -   no

force will come

            to me

up, now

    as   never before in my life,
as not

      at   20   or   30

I   am   in   a   depression, again

I hadn't felt such a   buoyancy

even at   12

with such force,

a   place   of

        nothing;
                        inside me   :   not even

a desire

                to be,   I'm,

                                low,

                                tired

such a life-breathing fullness inside

114

it is a new tiredness I know,
gripping me so strongly
I have no control over it as

me

        & I sing at   work, happy,

happy,

        as I never   have

                        been

I used to have over

                tiredness,

      a force

    as powerful as

my life force

           used to be

in   my   life   :   strong, a

           vital force

if I cannot write, create

I am finished, &

the depression

spreading that happiness, from

the vitality

the vitality

to the people in

is   frightening to me, a

meaningful weakness, presaging

                        my   death

        the Lab -   I push open the

        door, flipping it open with

        the strength of my wrist

: I told   Jackie

                        when

she came home today

                  about   another depression:
            I told her   never

                              to have a

      gun

            in the house   .. I am
                        too close
                              not, at some time,
                  to want

                              death...

      & leave the Lab with a
                        rush
                  of vital force
                        which   I feel

                  at 48 –

            a   raw   power

            a   Freedom ,

my age ,   death is

coming

it   is   inevitable . .   I   am

an   ageng

man.

a freshness   ,   exuberance   . *yes!*

I   am moved   forward   by my life,

I cannot die,

I   love   being.

(don't I ?

3.

on, the, moon. Then
from earth. *creation:*
human beings. walk there.
away from earth planet,
as not usual. in fact:
not, breathing, the moon's
atmosphere -(to die there).
   moon   visitors
as if moving around on
the place.
          as if to be
on the moon for the first
time/on, the, moon: so
human, 2 men awkward
with little gravity (not,earth)
LUNAR MODULE in
shadows, Armstrong
and, there, in the distance,
of space, and, time, sight
earth.   in dark
space
that, planet. away.away,
from earth, in space,Moone,
in space, both in the dark
     space yes, and
certainly distant:yet, held
together, thru a force
in time/moving
    earth/and the moon were
in movement/and the 2 men
were awkward (spacesuitd)
   walking;
on the moon: TV,in the den,
   speaking to earth (natives),
human. Outside earth's
bounds

[effect   - *visitor's*
 mind]
Yes, outside earth's blue-
green oceans, trees, there
in the space, white &

                  blue,
BALL,earth,in space, and

to return
to the (native) earth from
the (circling earth,
  earth, sun) -
in the galaxy in space

distant of other galaxies.
in, space,
     such in continuous
     movment,in,space,so.
of moon then walk, Neil &
Buzz - hook up
               Columbia
               to return
away from the moon to
that planet there in space

dark,Distant,off: off:
  VISITORS FROM SPACE
Away. Space, visitors,
to
the moon/from the earth.
into...
          Voyager 1,11..
               (minde-
  VISITORS FROM SPACE
   to, MooNe, a *creation*
outside earth/ outside th/
earth [outside the earth]&,

          space, visit?

certainly distant,*earth/itis:*
               on,the,moone:

howd universe be created.
when, urth, then. *so moone.*
why why what. why.
YES AT THE DISTANCE FROM
CREATION ON THE MOONE THEN,

this is the universe distans

```
        interlocking gears teeth engaging teeth &
      moving NOISE, gears in moving logs bang
       bang sharp bang rolling huge barrel logs

          moving inside banging sharply against inside
  IRON  WALLS  water, inside, flushing out, wood
                   tumbling inside barking drum
              rotating ROTATING sharp NOISES
     continuously/noise-rotation SHARP SHARP
                                    bangs,
        iron barking drum barking logs water soften
      bark scraping logs together/tumbling
                              inside BANG BANG
            BANG
            BANG     iron sides/moving
                  continuously, bark shavings leaking
        outside
    the barking drum MOVING MOVING sharp sound bang
          against/against (unnerving) logs moving
            continuously
                against the iron BANG CONTINUOUS
        gears interlocking gears, belts moving
                              gears/IRON
    LOGS    (alone in the noise UNNERVING) BANG
    BANG

         BANG/BANG/sharp noise  iron side
      iron barrel moving on its side BANGlog
    again, banging CONTINUOUSLY the BANGING

  against the IRON. barking drum-ROTATING/ROTATING!

                              banginhuman,BANG.
                               BANG,fuck
        fuck.
```

```
       Alone, the young man, in the old wood room, the
    Island Division wood room.
```

the barking drum rotating logs banging of the sides of the
rotating barking
drum, logs tossed around inside the drum water sprayed inside
the barking

drum, bark of logs wet softened, chipped cut banged by the
sides of the barking drum rotating the logs banging against
        the iron sides of the rotating drum & bark
strips, peelings pressed outside the drum
        shoveled wet bark strips into the wheelbarrow
        as well as the sawdust, swept
beside the rotating iron drum continuously banged
 by the logs rotating inside the iron drum
   rotating continuously, so the man alone
            with his thoughts shoveling & sweeping
            beside the continuously rotating barking
   drum, bark peelings/strips & sawdust, logs
    peeled, whitened logs wet on the conveyer belt but in the
basement alone
the old wood room, moving belts & old iron gears, old wet black
continuously moving canvas belts moving gears into gears
moving

            the old conveyer belt-iron barking drum upstairs
water dripping from continuously moving
barking drum & continuously spraying water into the basement
    shoveling bark peelings away from the moving belts/
struggling with the heavy wheelbarrow/wet peelings, shoveling
    sawdust away from the moving belts & moving
    gears in the darkened cellar logs
            banging water dripping into the damp cellar wet
cement stone walls logs
banging in the iron barking drum overhead continuously, alone
in the noise, the silence of the noise continuous a young
man
 in torn sweatshirt & dungarees, boots wet alone in the
basement of the old wood room bare light bulbs over
the moving belts & planks damp wet on the
dirt water in puddles up the stairs on

the wooden steps from
the dark dank cellar, the wooden hand rail a smooth wood
        rounded a hand rail by human hands, very smooth, soft
in the young man's hand, so that along
the conveyer belt
                leading to the iron barking drum
continuously rotating, banging logs two
 men with hand picks, sorting logs to split, pulling on oversize
logs into the splitter/into the rotating
                            drum on the conveyer
                        belt, banging logs
        banging logs continuously of logs
 in the old wooden & brick wood room, the two men working &

talking loud to each other
    while the young man moved alone in the wood room
to the bark peelings shoveling continuously
   sawdust sweeping as the iron barking

drum rotated, rotated logs inside barking logs against logs
& iron sides striking off bark continuously bangs, bangs,
sweeping & shovel bark peelings alone in his silence
with the noise in ears & water, damp

            EARTH on knees
      scratching
           in the dirt,
           for
                 weed, digging

      out
          the green leaved weed,
               grass

        no tool for digging:
          fingers
              dirt stained

          (sun hot on my back)
        scrubbing on my knees
          for weeds, *not*

           standing
       among the blue leaved cabbages,

```
twisted
            on my knees
    weed, snapping
    the stalk off
    and
scratching down
            into the dirt
    and small stones
    for rooted


        weed, rough dirt
    under knees, bending
        over carrot delicate
            tops


        carefully pulling
        at weeds
            moving along on


        my knees in the dirt
        across the earth
    among
    leaves, tomatoes, cabbages,
        bean plants, carrots
            and broccoli
            digging
                    hand into
                    earth, naturally


    weeds, dirt rough/stones on knees



in the darkened aisles of books, feeling
```

grew in the boy's mind, behind eyes watched
Roy Rogers and Gene Kelly, Donald
Duck and Mickey Mouse,
Babe Ruth, Ty Cobb, Walter Johnson
and the Washington Redskins, eyes-
seeing-mind
Rembrandt-
chiaroscuro;
as, little boy

he'd seen emptiness (death) darkness of life,
so, too, Rembrandt in the ghetto,
defeated, created, with his mind, human,
paintings, eyes
of a man
enveloped

by thick darkness, and finally, wasted
flesh, age, still the boy saw

the human eyes real in the
darkness unmoving
eyes and darkness

endured, the human, fully developed mind
in Rembrandt's eyes.

unflinching

seeing, mind, itself: HUMAN

a "seed"

in the boy's mind,

books, pictures, but words

of a creative man

tenacious with his mind alone:

(a vision)   in Rumford, book

to read

.words, on paper, boy, and quietness, in
the walls, book lined wood dark
shelves. in the half light

ideas/feeling,

"loosened"

RULE DESTRUCTION BEGAN

and, darkness, failure

darkness, darkness, darkness, darkness, from inside the boy's
mind

I do not know what I am doing.   I do not know what I am
doing with this creation: I know you would feel better if I
could tell you that I do know: you'd feel that the creation
was more valuable as a human document - if I wrote that I had
control, knew exactly what I was creating - you'd feel much
more certain of the word's value -   I don't know what I

128

am doing because I don't have control over my creativity. I
was created. I do not control myself. I do not control my
creation. This creation.   I created: I create.
I do not want to know what I am doing: I do not want to try
to control the outcome of this creation: I seek to be in
harmony with creation. I do not oppose creativity – the work
of the creation. I seek to create. I do not know
where I am going with this creation. I create: I must create
continuously.   I cannot, then, tell you what I am doing.
      I cannot tell you what I am creating. This is
creation. Since I am a human being – only a minor part of
creation – one day you will discover this creation as a
creation. One day
you will understand that some of what I create here is
half-true, some certainly false – because I am a minor part
of creation – created. Do not accept everything I have
created here. Do not accept everything I have created here.
I am created

DO NOT BELIEVE

.Create –

4.

And I walk past Carlton Ames' little house - used to be the
    Forney's - old Mrs. Forney had flowers in her front yard
when I first came to see Jackie - behind a fence - she was
    very small, bowlegged, she waddled - her son was nicknamed
"Flash", worked in the Beater Room, a real ladies' man, a
    real drinker too, very short with thick glasses - he lived
with his mother in the little house - now the place a kind
of junkyard with the Ames - the wife had a small place for
odds and ends on the Dixfield road - and the old man
collected anything that might sell, old stuff no one wanted,
didn't matter what it was - piled it in the yard and on the
porch -their lights on, the windows of the small house warm
in the night - and in the dark sky, the moon, round, more
"palpable" to my mind because human beings had walked on the
moon, and I shivered - in my mind I was on the moon - there,
    so real, physical, to me in the night - turning, I saw the
warm lights in the windows of my home, the moon in my mind
    still, in the night sky - "palpable" - and two human beings
walking on the moon, in space - I felt my self to be
    in the space of the Milky Way galaxy - in my mind - the
moon, in my mind the space of the galaxy, and the space of
    the Universe - Earth - and the Ames' home, the Fallons'
home here, in Rumford - I looked at the moon in the night
sky and I knew I was in space: *the Universe in my mind -
[change the world] - to be,* ON THE MOON -
                                    *Goddamit I have to go to
work in that fuckin paper mill. Lunch basket heavy in my
                                    hand. Book, manuscript.*
(Home behind). Letters, words, on paper: make paper. THE
ORANGE LIGHT OF THE PAPER MILL, IN THE VALLEY, OVER THE HILL,
ABOVE THE TOWN, IN THE DARK: THE STEADY WHINE OF THE MACHINES
SOUNDING IN THE NIGHT AIR.   [an alien in space...on the
moon]. "JESUS CHRIST, I HATE THE HATE OF THAT FUCKIN MILL!"
                    *but, my security, in my lunch basket,
the manuscript, the creation there, to be worked on if the
work load is light tonight, if I don't have too much paper*

testing tonight, I can reread the work I've created, rethink and if I can't read I'll stop at my lunch basket a few times during the shift to open it and look at the manuscript, my creation, then go back to work, think about what I've written, let what I've written move around in my mind, my consciousness and my unconsciousness, as I test paper, stand at the Elmendorff Test Machine doing tears, let my self move in the creation, secure in itself, in movement, the creation moving inside my self, back and forth from my consciousness to my unconsciousness, taking notes if need be on slips of torn test paper, my self always moving in this creation in the Quality Control Lab, letting my self go, moving in the creation freely, working on the manuscript in my self, testing paper and creating, I will be near the creative "thing" throughout the night, connected to the creativity in the thing I am creating, I will be near my lunch basket, I will be able to look at the manuscript
and work, I'll be able to work and create, make money and
be alive.

My self will be alive. [Reta saved my life (after Jackie
saved my life) with her loyalty to family - I never
returned/joined her family - I resisted her love, I
resisted the family. I resisted home.]
Because I wanted death.   Walking.
over   [..do not enter with....]
She loved humanly.

yes, i do(Now   Live ,   in the Universe...) I no longer
think on the earth.

WYSIWYG

The Change of the Century

Work. Human beings went to the moon. And, human beings
made paper, books. The paper printed, bound paper pages,
  into a book. Read: intellect. Learning many people over
the years – centuries – from the books, increased, then
      knowledge, with the mind's use of the human knowledge
printed on the paper, in the books. Questioning. Work. We
  human beings, on the earth, so recently created in time,
living in trees, and in caves, reading words, ideas, facts,
understanding, but seeking more knowledge, different ideas,
facts, searching with "literary" minds, now – for paper, as
      far as we human beings know, presented to the Chinese
Emperor Yuan Hsing by the eunuch Ts'ai Lun, in the year 105
A.D. (Probably a more important date in human civilization
than the birth of Christ.) Paper in China, made by hand,
one paper sheet at a time, the paper makers; dried one sheet
of paper at a time in the sun's heat. Work. On earth, the
heat from the sun drying paper. The bark of trees, hemp
  waste, cloth rags, fish nets, macerated to fibers by hand
with mortar and pestle, mixed, then, with water, the water
  and fibrous matter poured on a square of coarse cloth, (a
mould), the water draining through the cloth of the mould,
  the wet fibers crossing each other to be dried on the mould
in the sun. (Or, dip the mould in a wooden vat of macerated
fibers and water, raising it up so that the fibrous matter
      lays on the mould, with the water draining back into the
vat.) This was work. Individual sheets of paper drying
  on the moulds in the sun light. Strip the paper from the
mould, use the mould again to make another sheet of paper.
Not changed, this process, work, in the 20th century, even
though a machine, at high speed, makes a paper sheet of a
      great width, rolling it up on a spool, still a sort of

Paper, newsprint - Sunday newspaper: The new theory of galactic

133

And then we know three human beings from the earth here will be
going to the moon the moon 238,000 miles from the earth and they
will fly. the human beings will fly in the air through the air
around the earth into space black space and move away from the
earth's gravity, rocketed out of the earth's gravity and into
space rocketed then into the moon's gravity to land on the moon
and walk on the moon for the first time 238,000 miles from the
earth, in space, and walk on another space object in movement
other than the earth the moon. and the human beings look at the
earth in the spaceship spacecraft moving away from the earth in
space seeing the earth in space lit up by the sun's light and
they rocketed into space through space toward the moon their
flight three days away from the earth to land on the moon.
seeing the moon the human beings from the space ship, moving away
from the earth in the space of the universe we know. moving
closer to the moon away from the earth away from the earth. this
is the Apollo XI spacecraft the human beings were moving through
space inside from which the earth was visible and the moon moving
farther farther from the earth than the moon as they moved closer
to the moon, the three human beings inside the spacecraft which
was constructed on earth and they were speaking to the earth as
they moved through space in the spacecraft: outside the earth's
atmosphere in space through which the men were traveling: Buzz
Aldrin, Neil Armstrong, Mike Collins. this was the trip to the
moon. this first move to the moon, to walk, human beings, on the
moon's surface, land and walk on the moon the human beings from
the earth live on the moon after flying three days 238,000 miles
from the earth measuring the moon's place for a landing three
days away from the earth the revolution of the moon, landing on
the moon, landing on the moon in the Lunar Module Neil Armstrong
and Buzz Aldrin as Mike Collins moved around the moon the two
human beings landed the Lunar Module and away from the landing
place in the Sea of Tranquility on the moon hidden from the
landing moon the two human beings landed the Lunar Module and

streaming motion will be a controversial topic at next month's confere

mould is used, moving, so that the water is shaken out of
    fibrous matter, and the paper is dried by passing between
heated cylinders - no change yet; but wood, reduced to
fibers, is used as a raw material for most of the paper made
today. Paper made faster, on earth, by machine, now, made
    to make money for stockholders in a paper company: using
technology, knowledge learned from books and research,
    experiments, trial and error, or practical experience, to
make better paper, paper cheaper, paper for many different
                uses; not more beautiful than hand made paper.
The major change in papermaking on earth: invention of the
        machine, machines. More, not necessarily better paper.
(And, papermaking spread from China: to Samarkand, 751 A.D.
    the papermaking craft kept secret by the Chinese, here
revealed by Chinese prisoners of war; Baghad, Harun al
    Rashid introduced paper with Chinese artisans; 900 A.D.,
paper made for the first time in Egypt; 950, Spain; Morocco,
                Constantinople, 1100; 1228, Germany; 1276,
Fabriano, Italy, paper mills; 1349, France near Troyes;
1420-70, papermaking introduced from Samarkand into Kashmir,
India; Poland - 1491; 1495 - first paper mill established in
    England by John Tate; and 1575-80, Mexico, 1576, Russia;
Dalry, Scotland, in 1591, and in 1690, America, William
            Rittenhouse established a paper mill in Germantown,
Pennsylvannia; 1731-4, a paper mill at Falmouth, in Maine.)
OK, inventions, discoveries - the desire for change, in the
human being, the new, creation, the solution to a problem -
    practical or intellectual - experiment, invent. On earth.
Work. So, in a sense, work, papermaking on earth changed,
    or advanced, from a handmade craft to a mechanical craft,
so that the amount of paper made became the purpose, the
money to be made, from the production of paper, the purpose.
Significant paper making inventions and discoveries on
        earth: after Ts'ai Lun in 105 A.D., Tso Tzu-yi improved

of relativistic astrophysics in Chicago. In the 1970's, instruments on

away from the landing place in the Sea of Tranquility on the moon
hidden from the landing as the spacecraft Apollo XI from the
earth moved behind the moon into the darkness away from the
sunlight on the backside of the moon was the man alone and into
the sunlight beside the moon moving, on the day from the earth
measure human beings' measure of July 20, 1969 the two earth
human beings men walked on the moon for the first time two earth
creations we think moved in the weak gravity of the moon, in
their suits to protect them from an air with little oxygen as the
spacecraft also moved around the moon and rocks were collected
from the moon to be returned were returned to earth and placed in
the LM to be joined to the spacecraft with the two human beings
from earth to return then after the walk on the moon away from
the blue planet earth, the men Buzz Aldrin and Neil Armstrong,
with Mike Collins, to be, then moved to the earth by the rockets
rocketing them to the sunlighted earth in space a blue and white
globe in the distance with the moon giant near after and before
the landing on the moon the walking humans there the surface of
the revolving space object around the earth 238,000 miles from
the earth. they went. we know. spoke and the photos of the
moon with their voices were transmitted relayed human voices to
the earth human beings waiting and listening watching looking at
the photos of the moon and the human beings, with the earth then
there, hearing from the moon the spacecraft Apollo XI stepping
outside the LM to the moon's surface in space, a human voice
human speech from earth on the moon now barren landscape moon
hearing Neil Armstrong with Buzz Aldrin there from space from
moon. see, in space, from the earth, then, camera made invented
on earth by the human beings the men seen who had landed on the
moon, Apollo XI, LM, constructed on the earth to be rocketed to
the moon to be heard via radio invented on earth from the moon's
surface as well as moving through space as well as moving through
Mike Collins heard on earth from the moon's surface, spoke, human
speech, human voice human voice heard radio transmitted 238,000

U-2 airplanes and high flying balloons enabled astronomers to measure

papermaking around 150 A.D. According to Chinese records,
about the year 300, paper became universally accepted as a
substitute for bamboo, wood and silk, for writing. 700:
paper first sized with gypsum, later with glue or a gelatine
made from lichen. About 1035, waste paper was repulped, and
again used as a papermaking material. 1151 - in Spain,
Xativa, a stamping mill for the maceration of rags. Adopted
from the Orient. Probably the earliest use of animal sizing
for paper used in Europe around 1337. And in 1540, the
glazing, or pressing-hammer, was introduced in Germany,
taking the place of burnishing paper by hand, as in the
Orient. 1680 - the "Hollander", or beater, invented in the
Netherlands, used for macerating papermaking materials.
Pressing hammers give way to wooden glazing rolls for
finishing paper with a smooth surface. And the discovery of
China clay by William Cookworthy, England, in 1733. Clay
was subsequently used for "loading" paper about 1807; by
1870, the use of clay for loading was a common practice.
1760, Jacob Rittenhouse, invented slanting plates in the
beater for macerating rags. And in 1764, George Cummings
was granted an English patent for the coating of paper.
This "coating" was composed of white lead, plaster of Paris,
stone lime, mixed with water. Karl Wilhelm Scheele, a
Swedish chemist, in 1774, discovered chlorine, which was
later used for bleaching paper stock. The hydraulic press
was invented in England by Joseph Bramah, 1790. It
supplanted the ancient screw press for pressing water from
new-formed paper sheets as they were held between felts.
1793 - English patent for heating papermaking vats with
steam granted to William Scott and George Gregory.
Previously, the vats had been heated by individual charcoal
burners. And, in this year, also, the earliest patent was
given in America for improvements in papermaking moulds by
John Carnes, Jr., of Delaware. Here, now, the very first

wave-length of the "left-over" Big Bang creation radiation and more

135

miles the speech of earth moving around the moon and the moon of
the two human beings walking working joking as on earth to be
cursing too on the radio from here. and, the earth, then, there,
here, seen from the spacecraft orbit. and the second orbit of
the earth by the spacecraft 18,000 MPH when the
Saturn rocket third stage engine thrust the three human beings
into space to be toward the moon toward the moon at 25,000 MPH
three men in sealed bubble helmets and pressure suits breathing
pure oxygen in the weightlessness of space, the command module
Columbia of the space traveling to the moon and Mike Collins
separated Columbia Saturn the rocket to fly attach the lunar
module Eagle to the Command Module attached to separate Saturn
from the LM and the CM to orbit the sun and Mike Collins rotated
the spacecraft in the hot sunlight slowly to prevent heatup or
freezeup away from the sunlight in the heat of the sun as the
earth slowly began to shrink in the CM's window moving away from
the earth as the earth slowly began to shrink in the CM's window
moving away from the earth, really bright blue of the ocean and
the white of cloud the earth as it is seen from space and really
bright blue of the ocean and the white of cloud the earth as it
seen from space between the earth and the moon with the
spacecraft moving away from the planet earth blue at the speed of
25,000 MPH toward the moon orbiting the earth itself orbiting the
sun with the moon directed for the place where the orbiting moon
would be in two days the three human beings. slowly, shrinking
sized earth, the spacecraft Columbia in movement with the Lunar
Module for a moon landing by human beings Neil Armstrong and Buzz
Aldrin on the next day transmitting photos television to the
earth from 130,000 miles, of earth in space, and the moon away in
the constant sunshine of the space between earth and moon moon
and earth then: third day the sphere of the moon filled Columbia
spacecraft's largest window third day the sphere of the moon
filled Columbia spacecraft's largest window. bluish glow of the
moon was earth shine, sun reflection large craters, sun

accurately measure the earth's and Solar System's direction and speed.

paper machine was invented, by Nicholas-Louis Robert, a
French citizen. The small, undeveloped machine, was set up
in the Essonnes paper mill, and the French government
granted Robert a 15 year patent and advanced money for the
perfection of the machine. Little more was accomplished by
Robert however. Mattias Koops, living in London, began his
experiments in the use of straw, wood and the de-inking of
paper. His work is the foundation of today's paper
industry. Rosin sizing - Moritz Friedrich Illig, in 1800.
John Gamble, on April 20, 1801, received the earliest
English patent pertaining to the paper machine: The patent's
title: "An invention of making paper in single sheets
without seems of joining, from one to 12 feet and upwards in
length". Gamble's paper machine was described as "a sheet
of copper (screen) joined at both ends, passing round two
cylinders, forms an endless web, and this receives the pulp,
which, travelling along, passes between two cylinders. The
paper is afterwards wound from between the cylinders upon a
wooden roller, which, when loaded, another is substituted
in its place without stopping the machine". The paper was
dried in lofts, as had been done previously with hand made
paper. The mechanical agitator, or "hog", for the agitation
of papermaking fiber in the vat was introduced in England
around 1802. Now, the name of Fourdrinier on the invention
list: A patent taken out by Henry Fourdrinier, July 25,
1806, states: "A number of moulds, of the description
called laid and wove, are hooked together to form one long
mould. A platform to hold the said moulds shall slide along
backwards or forwards, but in no other direction. A vessel
or trough from which paper stuff or material is caused to
flow upon the moulds through holes, each provided with one
or more registers to limit or mark the flow of stuff. A set
of cylinders, upon which is passed in the manner of a jack
towel, an endless web of felting. There is a third cylinder

When these two motions were calculated, a new fact was discovered: the

reflection large craters. and around the moon firing Columbia's
rocket engine to slow down for the orbit of the moon to disappear
behind the moon never seen from the earth was this moon surface
of highlands scarred by the meteorites of a billion years, a
billion years. and this was the movement away from the earth for
the first time outside the gravity around the earth and into
space of the three of three human beings, two human beings to be
walking on the moon sealed in pressurized suits and bubble
helmets around the moon so that the landing, sixty miles from the
moon's surface and in space the gravitation of the moon the
spacecraft Columbia orbiting as the three men slept for the day's
work in space to be. separation in the LM from the Columbia, to
land on the moon leaving Mike Collins in the orbiting spacecraft
to await their return to the LM to the Columbia spacecraft
orbiting the moon. so that the takeoff from the earth by the
Saturn rocket's five first stage engines; propulsion into orbit
around the earth began. no longer confined to the surface of the
blue planet in space but beyond, and to the moon's surface within
three days; flight of the rocketed spacecraft for the first time
to stand on the moon away from the earth in the universe, away
from the earth in the universe, separated. and to look back at
the earth to look forward at the earth from the bubble helmet
from the spacecraft that the three human beings see the earth
that blue planet shining white cloudscape and blue oceans in the
space of darkness when television in living rooms on the earth
238,000 miles away in space the moon's landscape earth with the
astronauts, the two human beings who were men, Neil and Buzz
human on the moon and away from their birthplace on earth in
space, in the universe walking on the moon's earth there in space
photographing back relaying the photos of the human beings and
the earth and the moon back to the human beings in their millions
on earth sitting in front of their television sets in their homes
and in Rumford, watching watching the relayed photos from the
238,000 miles back to the earth from that moon the object, in

Milky Way was being swept through space at 400 miles per second. Data

in contact with one of these cylinders, and this third
cylinder communicates by means of another web of felt with
an additional pair of pressing cylinders. When the moulds
arrive at the first cylinder, the felt web takes off the
paper and conveys it to the first pair of pressing
cylinders, whence it proceeds to the second pair, and
afterwards to any fit place of reception, so that continuing
the process, paper of amy length may be made, and with
separate moulds". August 14th, 1807, additional
improvements were made to the machine by Henry Fourdrinier
and his brother Sealey. (Today's paper machine, basically
the same as in 1806, is called the "Fourdrinier paper
machine".) To work, on earth, then, these machines and
discoveries for paper making: So, 1810, was probably the
date that the Fourdrinier paper machine was perfected, after
work by John Gamble and Bryan Donkin of England. And in
January of 1813, the paper machine was put into use on
commercial basis - a new age began for paper making. In
America, a cylinder paper machine, not the Fourdrinier
machine, was operated in the mill of Thomas Gilpin, near
Philadelphia. This machine did the work of ten vats in a
hand-papermaking mill. Inventions: 1820 - Thomas Bronsor
Crompton, England, drying cylinders for the paper machine.
1823: gypsum (calcium sulphate) used for the first time in
Europe as a "loading" material. And, in 1824, the first
machine for pasting sheets of paper together, forming
cardboard, a patent granted to John Dickinson, inventor of
the cylinder machine. 1827, the first Fourdrinier paper
machine in America. Built in England by Bryan Donkin. It
was put into operation at Saugerties, New York, in the mill
of Henry Barclay, on October 24th. And the first
Fourdrinier paper machine was built in America at South
Windham, Connecticutt, and installed at the mill of Amos
Hubbard, Norwich Falls, Connecticutt. Bleach, invented by

collected on the velocity of hundreds of elliptical galaxies in relation

space in space. where the human beings were walking on the moon
the object, were away from the earth in space as the human beings
on the earth were watching television in their living rooms in
their homes on the blue planet earth in space away from the moon
away from the moon, with the movement of the spacecraft through
space propelled rocketed into space of the universe were many
human beings from the earth with the photographs and especially
moving closer to the moon close to the moon and around the moon
the place scarred by meteorites of a billion years and never seen
from the earth then, at the time Aldrin and Armstrong, Buzz and
Neil maneuvered the LM toward the moon landscape earth and
settled down in the Sea of Tranquility there off the landscape of
the earth to be in space finally with the Voyager I and Voyager
II spacecrafts flying through space and farther than the moon
away from the earth then, and the moon to be to pass by the other
distant from the earth (in the solar system) photographing
Jupiter and Saturn and Uranus and the moons, testing the
environments of the planets testing flying moving passed the
planet Uranus into the space, into space, human eyes, intellect
far beyond the blue planet earth and the moon the moon hurtling
through space (of the solar system) and the universe away from
the earth relaying photographs of Jupiter and Saturn and Uranus
with information to the earth human beings with intellect off the
earth, away from the earth at 1,838,000,000 miles from the earth
1,838,000,000 miles from the earth in space with the human, with
the human as the moon became a place away from the earth with
Jupiter Saturn Uranus the moon became a place the earth's moon
one in revolution around the earth rotating and revolving around
the sun in the Milky Way Galaxy of the universe in space in space
away, in the universe, standing on the moon in the bubble helmet
and pressurized suit were Neil Armstrong and Buzz Aldrin
breathing pure oxygen, away from the earth standing and walking
on the solid moon in space revolving around the blue planet earth
in space speaking to human beings on earth who sat in their

to the Milky Way, produced an unexpected result: thousands of galaxies

Scheele in 1774, first used by American papermakers to bleach
rags. The "knotter" used for removal of knots and lumps in
        paper stock was invented in 1830 by Richard Ibotson of
England. 1831 - washing screens were used in the Hollander so
    that water could be constantly changed while washing paper
stock. Earliest use of drying rolls on a paper machine in
    France,in the Firmin Didot mill, 1833. Improved drying
cylinders for the paper machine invented and patented by
    Robert Ranson, in 1839. 1840 - Friedrich Gottlob Keller, a
weaver of Saxony, picked up a patent for a wood grinding
    machine. Keller's work was no doubt based on the practical
        experiments of Mattias Koops. (Perhaps, paper could be
considered a sacred material for human beings - if they could
    recall the feeling of sacredness today. It was considered
sacred by the Japanese - of value to Americans, not sacred -
Europeans, yes the Russians, Africans, South Americans, yes
everyone - to be valued - held sacred - for its usefulness to
human beings. [Seldom do we consider, in the 20th century, a
crafted material, an activity, a human being, sacred - very
    seldom does this attitude appear in today's human reality -
modern civilization - yet, paper, paper is of such great value
    to all, to every human being...] Not, simply, because paper
can make money for paper companies, stockholders, the paper
        workers - feed all - but because it can be used for the
purpose of another very valuable human invention: words.
        And, in the making of books - [not, not necessarily the
limited editions, with hand-made inks and papers, old-style
        glues, hand set type] - which were written for aesthetic
reasons, for scientific reasons, for business, education, or
    just plain entertainment. For the reason that on earth we
have writing on paper, developing human minds, over centuries,
        to the point that human beings now can move away from the
earth, step on the moon, and move also into the Solar System -
    Voyager I and II - with information gathering spacecraft,
transmitting the information back to earth. The reason, on

a gigantic portion of the universe appeared to share our galaxy's speed

comfortable living rooms in space in their homes away from the
moon in space watching watching and listening to the human voices
and watching the photos moving pictures photos video of the men
on the moon there in space outside Neil and Buzz on the
television sets screens in the living rooms of our house in
Rumford then at Chapitis' on Spruce Street, only two kids, on the
moon solid away from the human beings away from the human beings
sitting in their living rooms in front of their television sets
in Rumford standing on the moon with the Voyager I and Voyager II
flying spacecraft to encounters with the planets away from the
earth and their moons away, then, then Jupiter, Saturn, Uranus
and beyond into space beyond into space into space of the Milky
Way Galaxy in the universe away from the planet earth near the
sun (of the solar system) in the Milky Way Galaxy in the universe
Apollo XI moved to orbit the moon, with Mike Collins orbiting the
moon and Voyager I and Voyager II headed into space with human
beings alert to the spacecraft's movements in space past Jupiter
Saturn Uranus Armstrong, Aldrin, Neil, Buzz, walking on the
moon's earth surface the moon earth stood. in space away, as
away outside the blue planet's living world natives walking after
flying away from the blue planet earth in space there in space,
away, away as. I to the universe possible 238,000 an
outsider 1,838,000,000 miles into space to be certain, the man
walking on the moon in space of the universe, in the universe.
three human beings will fly and move into blackness of space.
three days yes to walk on the moon's earth. to be always then
with the creation movement away from the earth: the man on the
moon. in the creation in the creation. and then we know the two
men returned from the moon and walked on the earth then, from the
moon. 238,000 miles from the moon the men will walk on the
earth. human beings fly 238,000 miles through space in space
flying rocketed into space from the moon to the blue planet in
space earth and walk after moving in space through space in the
spacecraft Columbia with Mike Collins, Neil and Buzz, Armstrong
and Aldrin will move through space toward the blue planet from

of 400 miles per second. This fact called into question a basic assumpt

earth, the human mind, developed by the use of paper through
the written word, can exist away from earth in space, to
know, and to feel, living in far Universe. Mind in the far
universe.)
1851 was the year that paper was first made from chemical
wood fiber, originated by Hugh Burgess and Charles Watt.
And, in the year 1856, aniline dye (Perkin's mauve) was used
to color paper. (By 1870, dyes of this type were common.)
1857 - experiments in the sulphite process for the
preparation of wood fiber were begun in Paris by Benjamin
and Richard Tilghman. About 1860, the original Jordan engine
for refining paper stock, was made by the Smith and
Winchester Company for the Boswell Keene Company, East
Hartford, Conn. Joseph Jordan invented the machine. 1864:
at Camden, Maine, a firm that became known as the Knox
Woolen Company, manufactured the first paper machine
felting. 1872 - Carl Daniel Ekman and George Fry, working
in England, continued experiments with the sulphite process.
And, in 1875, the first coating of paper on both sides by
Charles Gage, Springfield, Mass. 1884: sulphate pulp
invented by Carl F. Dahl. And two years before, the first
sulphite pulp was made in the U.S. on a commercial basis, by
C. S. Wheelwright, Providence, R.I. The Ekman process was
used. So, in 1887, John Mullen, of Fitchburg, Mass., made
the first paper tester. The Mullen tester is universally
used even today. 1896: Rumford Falls, Maine, the largest
paper machine in the U.S., with a wire of 162 inch width, 60
foot length. And so on, to the electronic age, in which
computerization, and other technological developments,
improved the efficiency of papermaking: no inventions
significantly changed the nature of the Fourdrinier paper
machine however.
*So that, perhaps, then, paper could be - I feel a particular
kind of elation while typing the inventions which improved
the making of paper - could be considered a sacred material*

of modern cosmology: that the universe was expanding evenly, and with

139

the moon, move toward the earth with the three men will walk on
the earth after landing on the earth in in space of the universe,
the Milky Way galaxy in the universe here the creation moving
orbiting the sun the blue planet and the moon orbiting the earth,
the planet earth in space, leaving the moon, walk now on the
earth planet here. as the LM docked with the CM Columbia Aldrin
and Armstrong with Mike Collins rocketed out of the moon's orbit
out of the moon's orbit and toward the earth toward the earth as
the blue planet of white cloud and blue ocean grew large and the
spacecraft moving closer closer to the earth planet the
planet of white clouds and blue oceans growing larger and the
planet of white clouds and blue oceans growing larger in the
window and the spacecraft landed on the earth in the ocean and on
the earth the blue planet in space the three human beings would
land on the earth in the ocean and the three human beings would
walk on the blue planet in space in space. not the moon the blue
planet is in space, in creation: the blue planet was in the
universe and the moon was in the universe and the three human
beings the two human beings were flying toward the blue planet
earth in the universe. with Voyager I and Voyager II flying, the
man on the moon there the man on the moon. in space. move
toward the earth then move toward the earth with the move toward
the moon and into space, Jupiter Saturn Uranus the planets out in
space of universe, the moon in space of the universe and moon was
outside the earth, away from the blue planet earth.

They fly.

We know.

only local, small variations. There are many competing theories

by human beings - and I work in a paper mill where making
paper is a hassle, a "ratrace", not a sacred activity - if
    humanity could recall that feeling of sacredness it has
repressed in the modern age. And the date of 105 A.D. might
    be considered as sacred to human beings, to intellectual
searchers and questioners, the adventurers, the knowers, on
    the seemingly insignificant planet - Earth - in the Solar
System, in the Milky Way Galaxy, in the Universe that we
seek to understand. Paper - Ts'ai Lun, in China, the year
105 A.D. And, 1969 A.D., the year a human being from Earth,
the planet, in the Universe - the human mind, "our" thought,
outside the Earth's environment for the first time
physically. Then, Voyager I and II, deeper into the Solar
System - into the space of the Universe. Away from Earth.
Not, possible, without the use of paper - the invention of
paper - books - made in an industrial paper mill during the
20th century. And to make money: for stockholders. Money,
for food. Work. On the earth, then, paper yes. The paper
    machine, for the first time, invented by a Frenchman,
Nicholas-Louis Robert, 1798 - a sacred event in the history
            of humanity, civilization, on the earth.
Maybe. And cancer, with paper, human intellect, to continue
investigations, to cure.
Read: intellect. Work. The paper machine invented,
(it was work for Nicholas-Louis Robert, in France, 1798.)
In space, the human mind a billion and a half miles from the
                earth, in space, near Uranus...
Information. The human intellect, human feeling, at work,
    in space. This is of the paper machine, will be, the
knowledge gained, saved, on paper, etc. Think. Every child
learns to read and write. Hand made paper.   Hand made.
Every child reads books, writes on paper. Paper is
        made with machines, today, yes, in Rumford, Maine.

on the structural formation of the universe, but none predicted the

We know.

Moving through space, then, the two men, walking on the moon.
Mike Collins, the man, orbiting the moon, going behind the moon
seeing the back side of the moon which no man had ever seen
before, orbiting the moon and thinking. I Tom Fallon think,
watching the man on the moon there, on the moon
away. Earth, away.

And Voyager, I see
near Jupiter Saturn Uranus flying by I see, and, think
here.   I am very near Uranus. I am very near
Uranus.
I think   and,   I. create.....as

HOW   do Human think/Speak - (how)do, HUMAN write   I,write:
200,000 MILES FRO M EARTH (in Space)With
   no gravity,with   little/ Gravity.
                  200,000,Miles
                     From   urth:human,

This is the moon.

large scale streaming motion which these calculations have posited.

IMPROVISATION #2

Outside (the library) WCW!

*For I confront peace, security, and all
the settled laws, to unsettle them.*

Walt Whitman

*...penetrate to the region of that secret place
where primeval power nurtures all evolution. There
where the powerhouse of all time and space - call it
brain or heart of creation - activates every function...
In the womb of nature, at the source of creation...*

Paul Klee, from *On Modern Art*

1.

i walk
    Around the corner. of Essex avenue,
    bright lights of the mill
    the orange pink shock   (i stop)

of the mill's lights in the darkness as
                            i stood with my lunch basket
in hand, standing in the street sidewalk
covered snow high snowbanks.
the mill rose into the sky
above me brightly lighted a square sharp
    angle

    building/smokestack/Smoke streaming into the Darkness

    highlighted by the orange pink lighting
                                    the night cold,
        clear, the air fresh (no wind) snow
white and the street snow packed
        under my overshoes feet, fresh air in the night

darkness going to work in the mill down Essex avenue:
        ugly building, ugly lights, Hate   (violence
        i stood on the snow-covered
            street, *between my home & the mill work
        my self, yes into -*   (mixed
                                    emotions
            & Thoughts,,   STAND, on
                            the snow packed
                            street
in the cold air, bright, harsh orange pink   SMOKE   SMOKE
Lights   on the metal   SQUARE
                    mill buildings/Smokestacks

                              a SMOKE
                                 SMOKE
in my human eyes/sound,machine,onesound   whine
              monotonous/continuous
                              &,in my human ears
                    OUTSIDE   THE   PAPER   MILL
              (where I work, 11-7 tonite, master -
                         OUTSIDE   OUTSIDE

                                        THE   PAPER.

        tom

                         loom,inside :do not go.

                                   Cezanne. do not
                                      go
here i stand in the night air here i stand in the night air here
i stand in the night air here i stand in the night air

    here i stand in the night air here i stand in the night air
    here i stand in the night air here i stand in the night air
                         here i stand in the night ai

                              - Strike over
                    smoke over the angles/streaming into
            the Darkness orange & PINK lighted SMOKE streaming
                    into the night above the paper mill
                         into my self, tom;   strike,strike
    & more beauty!   *(shiver*

        (pink)   O R A N G E   O R A N G E   S M O K E

        O R A N G E   S K Y   :O R A N G E   S K Y   (blaze-)

notebook 3x5 in
my back pocket, words
notes, ideas
sentences
a boy in the air force a
notebook, writing
notes, asking
questions
continuously
confused,
notes, questions
life-questions
what was the meaning
of life, nonsense
to me
a kid "turned off"
by society's conformity,
injustice. on page
after page scribbled
words barely
legible,
speculations of reality,
half-formed thoughts
my solidity

     to protect
        me from the death I fear so much:
       the death
         of my consciousness

   the thin paperback book with its creative writing
    - human words on paper - with
       the 1st part of the 2nd improvisation folded into
      the page facing part 1 of the 1st improvisation - two
  creations to protect me from non-creation,
           the death

```
        of my self - literature I created
                                from a risk of my consciousness
                        in death - the unconscious
                                and the words on paper
        I created words on paper from my risk with death,
        my mind moving within death, anarchy, chaos, of my creation
                                        for the creation
                        to become a reality  (so charteng


                "uncensored paper mill" in my pocket


                        in my jacket pocket the force
                                of creation to protect me
        from non-creation - on my person, in my pocket,
        the creation on a piece of paper, folded into
            the pages of a book, a protection from non-creation


        in my fear, living, the words created, living,
        protecting my mind from fear, chaos, death
        that I know threatens me every instant
            of my creation, existence - the creation
            from the source of creation, in my jacket
            pocket     standing on Essex avenue     secure
                uncertain     facing the mill orange smoke
                the night    death in the world there, within
        death I know, am familiar with, accept
                    as reality, creation with death natural, fear
                    natural,      charteng opening the possibility
                            of creation, the creative source/
            from death:        darkness, in my mind
                                        opening creation
            the source, exploding
                                with possibilities, as I
        balancing my consciousness in the unconscious
            the threat of my extinction possible, living
        with the threat, in fear, unnerved
                            by the balancing in death
            within my self within my own alien world
```

as natural, tentatively moving close
to death toward
    the creative source,   creation
                    creation threatening
with its force, my horror of being nothing here
- meaninglessness within me - death -
my very small human mind, exploding with
                    words
  sounds in the source of creation, anarchy
  rule
          consciousness, within the order
of reality/consciousness the creative source
             threatening
         consciousness the
force exploding continuously /charging reality/
  my unconsciousness charging my consciousness
    with possibility phenomenal threatening married
    with the creation only for an instant in explosion
  with the pure source / out, charteng - vitalized -
with death's reality in my self - Universe
  Horror - (creation   and the book

beside me in bed, the manuscript, near my fingers
to protect my self from extinction, created
  as I lay to sleep before 11 to 7 after
  supper, in fear, unnerved by creation
    with the paper, words typed on paper,
    words I had created from my connection
with the   source - in fear - to quiet

my anxiety, the feeling of the threat, to rest
  with this small part of the creation, (my creation)...

    in bed. waiting to sleep before work
          in the mill
        threatened by death
the darkness / the risk
  a darkness so frightening

                                        to me
        I am attracted to the dark
          I must live near the reality of death
                                    to see life/gain
life   I must live in annihilation   I must live
       in natural fear
              to live in reality   creation

            undefined   nebulous   unknown,
         in the unruly
                     unconscious, natural, I am
                                        drawn
        to the chaos
                  in my transconsciousness I knew
             the vitality
                        of my unconscious, the creation

        at its source   the force form at
                                its most pure
                                         primitive
              a catalyst of forces and forms
                                in outer reality
        exploding source
                    intuited through my transconscious
                        yielding
                                   my consciousness
          for creation, destroying, risking
                    charteng created here

          in my small self ,   creation
                                in my jacket pocket
        standing on the snow packed street
                              the sky smoke pink orange,
                        with the mill building
                                    ,cold air
          the book and the manuscript was in my pocket
                Words, human, here I thought
                        (death's reality a creation)...

I lay in bed with the book in the dark fearful, alone
very small, but with creation
     death with me
               (to be close to the source to be close to the source,
                    to be close to the source
                                        destroy

          sound of Ornette Coleman - altosax -
off-key - that's the
right sound -   abrasive - out-
          of-balance -   fits me -
    It's the destructive sound
               - the bastard -
     "cutting across"   (watch your soul)
                    give me that trumpet & that
                    violin,
sounds-noise.   cutting breath mind sound.
    Ornette music,   ((jazz   Cry.
                    cutting breath mind sound.
                              ALTOSAXOPHON:

150

```
        sound of Ornette Coleman - altosax -
off-key  - that's the
right sound  -     abrasive  -
     off-balance -  fits me -
  It's the destructive sound
    - (the bastard) -
  "cutting across"                FITS ME

            give me that trumpet & THAT
                   violin,                    sounds-noise.
                cutting breath mind sound.
   Ornette   music,      ((jazz       Cry.
                  cutting/breath/mind/sound/
                         ALTOSAXOPHON-
```

```
    sound of Ornette Coleman - altosax -
    off-key - that's the
    right sound -       abrasive - out
       of-balance -    fits me  -
      It's the destructive sound -

             - the bastard -
        "cutting across"
           give me that trumpet & that
                violin,
    sounds-noise.    cutting breath mind sound.
      Ornette  music,    ((jazz          a hate music, death
                             music, jazz Ornette!ALTO
                                      cutting sound,

            MONK / Mingus  - Coltrane -
        & Taylor -  Ayler,

                              COLEMAN -
                     Braxton,        COLEMAN:
   Monk:                       blood move
```

From despair, death, comes creation. I don't know why.
(I have always been very conscious of death.)

ax

br

ax

ax

Human art, begotten in death. Life, so, from death, darkness,
too. With the dogs for a walk along the road, ordinary woods and
a brook from Woodrowville, the swamp behind the house. The strike
is over. Bean Brook: water very slowly running out of the culvert,
into a pool-wide place, narrowing as the water moved away through
the leafless alders. A dark surfaced pool, the grey-dull barked,
thin trunk alders leaning over the water, no leaves, and I could
see into the woods, leaves on the ground tan-ochre-brown darkness
under the alders - (Arthur Arsenault had hung bird houses from
gray birches among the alders.) These ordinary trees. Two dogs:
Pepper at brookside for water, and Spice, off down the road
lickety-split. The pool almost black surface now, the grey barked
alders leaning over the pool, no green leaves to obscure the brook's
path through the small trees, and the pool, dark, stopped me,
standing at the culvert, I looked at the darkness, the black surface
of the pool, deep pool, now, I thought-felt, darkness, of life the
woods, drew my thought, feeling, and the grey and brown colors, I
walked away from the pool calling to Pepper. The hell with Spice,
I thought, I want to go into the woods now in death, in a darkness,
a natural death, a natural depth I knew existed here now as I
turned into the ATV path with its dull-green short grass leaf-covered
and tall ochre grasses, clusters against the grey alders, the death
in the woods with my feet on the earth: natural death, faded colors
of the woods beside the road I walked alone Pepper stepping lightly
ahead of me in the woods. For I knew the woods, death in the woods
for many years, a boy walking the woods alone. A place where I
would die, naturally, old, and the old goldenrod there, dark brown,
twisted leaves, flower tufted brown-white an ordinary death here,
many old goldenrod beside the path, old dark leaves dry in my hand
the stalk stiff, upright and thin. Comfortable dull, color brown,
nature - death it is. For my death, a death, natural, an art here
in reality - a woods, from the dark pool with no green leaves now,
and no intensity...no green. Walking here, and, with, human,
thought. And death is welcome, I feel: the pool, darkness, is

153

Scabs waiting in the Time Office to go home

I could have cleaned out the scabs with a machine gun

Every one of the scabs - I could've cleaned them all out at once
with a machine gun

I can't believe no one's lost it yet
I can't believe no one's lost it yet

We could sneak a pistol into the mill between shifts easy

And walk into the Main Office and start shootin
Clean out every one a them goddamn bastards in the Main Office

That's the thing to do - fuck the scabs - get the Big Shots!
We sat in the Lab drinking coffee at 3 A.M.

welcome. Asters are very tall, wild, but not blue colored, delicate petaled flowers, green leaf - brown and dry. Grey brown and white tufts of flower delicate in my eye, mind, with the pool's dark, drawn to death and its inscrutable nature, welcome, satisfying: brown, ochre, dull green, black color: I find the subtle contrasts satisfying of death in these woods near the very slow moving water, of Bean Brook. Death lures me. The end of things living in the woods around the brook.

Cold. Change in the weather: a five inch snow, and then cold. The first cold of the fall. And the woods, as I walk, a bleak landscape of leafless trees, muted browns and greys, snow on the ground. With the cold air. White snow over the grey brown ochre colored woods.

Shostakovich - the opening of the 11th Symphony - bleak, a sound subdued, slow movement, a quiet noise; thoughtful music. Lifeless, created. I play the 15th Quartet, and the opening of the 5th Symphony, the 11th's first movement over and over, now that Fall is here - now that I have seen the dark pool of Bean Brook. The impenetrable darkness, a lure for my mind - death a lure in the woods grey and brown. The life in death, in my mind, stimulated by the sight of the dead and dying natural world, seeking the woods, slowing my self into the natural death: the dark pool alluring, suggesting to my self a creative release. Death, in the 15th Quartet, an invitation for my creative source, "revelation", energy...darkness, dead, the end, the impenetrable, real. Opening up my mind...to the "hidden source" I feel in the dark water, under the black surface of the quietly, very slow moving water. Cello Concerto #2 - obscure - in its "darkness" - small, undrama - impenetrable music from Shostakovich - the weakness of human life - death, a living reality - death realized - death in existence, living - in the woods, in front of me, the dead, familiar. Natural. (Death in creative reality: death
in creation. The dead a reality,
in living creation. In my
mind, self, death, a known reality.

YOU STUPID SCAB! YOU THINK YOU GOT A GOOD
JOB - YOU WAIT TIL BOISE PUTS THE FUCKS TO
YOU BUDDY! The young woman shouted angrily at the bearded man
inside the car, spitting on the windshield.

11 - 7, in the Q. C. Lab
walking away from
the computer terminal
the words come
into my consciousness,
I am going to die -
I can't get out of it!
- (I'm afraid) - I will lose
my consciousness - I don't want to lose my
consciousness of this world. (I WILL DIE)
Fear.

(When I discovered sex, woman, I found that society
was insipid; the wild passion - reality - of life, nature
was better, more fulfilling, for my self. I was alive.)
Reality: STRIKE.
12:01 AM. Our paper mill, (Rumford)
shut down for the 2nd time in 6 years. reality. Strike
against Boise Cascade. We shut down the mill...!

I hate. Yes. Hate. Boise Cascade
hates. I hate: anger. Hate,
yes: hate; hate; hate; hate; hate.

Energy, of death, in the dead.
Impenetrable darkness alive.) Thought-
      provoking, in my self, the darkened
water pool: ordinary life.

"Picasso was a crazy bastard! I don't care what you say!
Hey, that cubist stuff - that first one, that was about
WHORES - now isn't that something - that's great stuff!"

"What the fuck was wrong with Picasso? Jesus Christ, look
what he created! Cezanne first started that shit - then
Monet - look at that nut van Gogh - look what they created!
They were crazy, shit-faced nuts, that's what I say fella!"

November 1:   and, in the afternoon, after the strike,
                                      the dogs with me to walk
                                    down the road, stop at the culvert water
                                    dark, slow moving, quietly, alders
                                      not leaved, bare small trees with
                                          grey bark: around the dark water
                                          and
                                    into the woods seeing, I let Spice go up
                                    the road alone, took Pepper back, smoking a
                                    cigar, walked into the woods on the path
                                        strewn with dead leaves, seeing
                                            into the woods, trees bare
                                    now,
                                          tall wild flowers, asters dry
                                        and dark brown, flowers feathery
                                        whitened, goldenrod a
                                            foot above me
                                          and brown leafy stalks
                                          beside the path with
                                            the furry whitened
         old leaves   flower
                                        beside a bramble, wine-red
                                        grey alders, thin trees
                                            in the woods here
                                        near the brown wildflower

Scabs
waiting in the Time Office
as I came off the footbridge I could've
cleaned out the place with a machine gun
I said sitting down for coffee
in the Lab,
every one of the scabs! (the strike over) I'm surprised
at least one of the 340 guys these scabs
put out of work hasn't gotten into the mill & shot up
the fuckin main office - it'd be easy
to bring a pistol into the mill
& shoot those bastards - not the
scabs - but nobody's lost it, not one!

Yeah, but I'd
like to - I'd like to lose it - I'd like to pull
a fuckin Rambo up at the rewinders! I'd like to clean out
the whole goddamn bunch of those filthy bastards -
I'd like to lose it just once!
3 A.M. November - after
the strike, we went back to work in September. SCABS
still in the mill & our agaony, 321 of "our people"
still outside I'LL TELL YOU WHAT
WE DID WE MADE A FUCKIN
MISTAKE
WHEN WE DIDN'T TAKE CARE A THAT 1ST BASTARD BOISE
HIRED WE SHOULDA HAULED HIM OUTTA HIS FUCKIN
CAR THE 1ST TIME HE CROSSED THE PICKET LINE
AN BROKE BOTH HIS LEGS THE HELL WITH THE COPS
WE HAD ENUF PEOPLE ON THE PICKET LINE - SHOOTIN
UP TRUCKS WAS A WASTE A TIME - WE DIDN'T SCARE NOBODY
THEY STILL WENT ACROSS THE PICKET LINE
agaony
WE SHOULDA HIRED SOMEBODY TO KILL ONE A THE BASTARDS THAT'S
WHAT! WE WERE JUST A BUNCH A PUSSYCATS AN BOISE

Fertility...fertilize. I want to fertilize. And I can feel the women

```
                                        stalks
                              bark of the trees grey
                                       with the muted
                              leaves' color, browns
                              of many shades on
                         the ground under foot, bare
                                          trees, bare
                                          trees and
                              the wildflowers brown,
                                flowers white, feathery
                                in the woods

                   late, in the afternoon, late in the day, the sky
                   a muted blue with the grey tree branches
                   a tangle for my eyes, brown leaves, light
               and dark, dry and goldenrod brown, tall, over
               me, wine-red bramble beside the path tangled
                         with brown aster, the water dark, slow

                         running
                                  alders over the brook water grey
                              and the afternoon very quiet,
                                       subtle colors
                                       of the woods
                                       and
                                  the dark surface, blackness,
                                  of the slow, quiet
                                             moving
old                                          brook
dead                                  brown, grey shades
leaves             of color, dead leaves and dead flowers
                              the bare limbed trees and dark
                                   water, the water

                                   impressed me, since

                                   i felt this muteness
                                   quietness, in myself
                         leaves
                         dead

               in the absence of vitality a vitality

                    a fullness,
                         an evenness of feeling
                    a subtle shade of feeling,
     i felt a unity with the old leaves on the earth under
        my feet, with the muted colors of the woods

                                   the
                                        absent vitality
                                        of the green leaves
                              i felt a unity with the dark
                                   water, sandy bottom
                                   now impenetrable
```

                              KNEW IT!
NOW WE GOT FUCKIN SCABS ALL OVER THE PLACE!   (Strike, agaony
        & good people on the outside replaced by Boise scabs/
union busters/40 year men, broke production records
            for the company
            young people just starting a family, 3rd generation
                              paperworkers, Rumford natives!
            FUCK BOISE CASCADE!
                        get rid of the scabs, we
gotta intimidate the scabs in the mill.
    We sat uneasily in the Lab, smoking, taking a break
    from paper testing at 3 A.M.   The strike was deep in our minds.
        (The strike of Local 900, UPIU, against Boise

                                        Cascade, at
the Rumford paper mill, ended
September 21st, and production is still down in the mill - BC
is lying in the press about production - because everyone
        is depressed, just going thru the motions.
(and in my mind the dark pool
            obscure, "inviting",
        contemplation: death, in reality, my death
        ...woods, brown leaves dried...
                "an invitation"
                        to be close to
                            the dying
            ...the black surface of the water
                        with the Shostakovich
                        15th quartet, also
                into
                in to
                    the death of things, here
                uselessness   has a form
                                and color, special

in the Lab.   Two women...three women...in the Lab...there is beauty...a

                    a transition   alive, death
                          and natural, easy
                    to accept, the grey, the brown,
                          the black, ugliness

                                         real,
                          [threatening] existence
                          real,
                    palpable the dry
                          brown, twisted
                                    leaf
                    of the goldenrod, death
                          palpable
                             in my fingers
                             leaf dust -
                          so in my mind
                             my unconscious

                                         death

                          reflected,
                                    alive there
(lay with the CANTOS, PATERSON
        MAXIMUS, THE BRIDGE,
        ULYSSES, THE WASTE LAND
      literature of my time,
             my language charged with creation in the books
        I lay close - my mind closer - to the maximus of
   creation there can be -)

"invited" by them...I feel the women, the woman, in the room, of the Lab,

160

dirty white

sensitive   shade,

        rough
            disordered   natural disorder of the
                                woods

                            greybirch
                                white birch, black
                                grey birch

                                unpretty
    unimpressive

                        bleak .   subtle
    death.

            I almost lost the relationship between my
                consciousness and my unconsciousness.
                            I was in pain.

around me. I am always surrounded by the women here. I feel the "waves

hurt yourself,

in, my notebooks, i find
        question - only question

        i find no answers - questions

                                        questions,
i have no final answers for

i am   scared   i write   i ask,

i know nothing, for certain   yes, i am
afraid: but i ask, continuously, repetitiously, questions

        i do not know   i do not know, i ask
(little notebooks, with words, questions)

        drink another bourbon, Old Crow, numb your self,
    hurt your self, get down, into death: numb your
      mind, yes: go down there, where you should not go, tc
see death, in reality, darkness, into the other world

from the women, around me, from their bodies, from their flesh, from their

```
                                              RUN
                                              RUN
                       GET AWAY FROM FALSE IDEAS
                                     "THE SYSTEM"
                                            DRINK
                                         STRAIGHT
STRAIGHT                      TO DESTROY "THE RULES"
                                             WALK
                             ACROSS THE LINOLEUM
                                            AGAIN
                                  THE WHISKEY,
                                     AND DRINK
                                  IN FRONT OF
                                   THE MIRROR
                            TIP THE SHOT GLASS
                                          UP,
                                          AND
                                  WATCH/POUR
                                 ANOTHER SHOT
                                          NOW
                                  STOP, STOP
                                   CONFORMITY
                                  STOP, STOP
                                          GET
                                     IN/SIDE
        waste

                          IN THE ROOM ALONE AFTER
                                          WORK
                                  IN THE MILL,
                                      NUMB IT
                                     NUMB IT,
                                       ERASE.
                                   CONFORMITY
KNOWLEDGE

                               CLOSE YOUR EYES
                               CLOSE YOUR EYES

femininity, in the Lab.  Here I am, next to this sexuality, every minute
```

163

                    the little boy in the Rumford library
                      took down MEN OF ART
                              and read of the human
                                    sacrifice
                        in the darkness of the soul,
                            death sought
                                          drinking
                                    Old Crow in Skunk LaFleur's
                                          one room rent
          working nights in the mill, always working nights
            in the Kraft Mill, the stink of chemicals
            in the Bleachery, strong, anti-human
            and it was true, that
                        in the darkness (of Rembrandt)

                        i could see
                              more clearly
                              life whole,
                        my self
                  in depth, a fulfillment
                              with sacrifice (hard) in
                        the movie house, the dark
                              French films
          L.I., Hempstead, of the Fifties   black & white
                        the grey life
                                    on the screen
                        feeling accepting life
                                    on the screen
                              human failure
                              (my self)

of the eight hours I am surrounded by their fertility, hear their feminine

                    In reality
              looking into
                          Rembrandt's eyes
                          in the dark
                    finally an old man,
                    his sadness

                                            human
alien to my every day
America,
              existence, Christ crucified in the etchings
                          an old man an old man with eyes
                    drinking Old Crow, a two-time
                          college dropout, a loser: DESTROY
APPEARANCES
only the dirt of the ghetto, as before
              no more costumes
                          of the exotic Orient
                    no wedding gowns, feasts
                          no magnificent officers of the guard
                    no more riches, only
                    the man, and the ghetto

                                the ghetto with the Jews
in Amsterdam   "last explorer of the spiritual" yes
        drink, yes, get down
                          inside,   lose eyes, boy,

voices, hear their sexuality, the "waves" of their sexuality in their

At the 1st Maine Festival, I naturally went into the Walker Art Museum, Bowdoin College. The vestibule - gypsum slabs, sculpted reliefs, from Assyria - and, cuneiform, carved in this stone - from Assyria: large areas of this relief, with majestic half-human, god-like figures, covered with cuneiform script. I could not resist touching the cuneiform carving - from Assyria - the first language in written form - human writing - in Maine.

I can see the carved stone script now, feel as I felt then, my hand on the script, on the cuneiform, the first written human language - the words of my ancestors - from Assyria - my fingers ran lightly across the cool stone, the straight, masterly carved cuneiform script. I can feel the tension from my hand to my shoulder, and in my stomach, as I then felt the ancient lettering of "my people", who had carved in stone the cuneiform script.

My "sacred" language - here in stone at Bowdoin College - from an ancient civilization, the first true civilization, from Assyria - venerable, to me, the ancient, first language in stone here. Across the centuries, the dead, speak to me of language, and the art of a written language, the masterful script carved in the gypsum, the art of a written language, and the minds of human beings searching for knowledge, counting their material possessions, recording their activities and recreating their ideas and feelings, impressing these first in clay - not on paper because paper did not exist - on small clay tablets - and preserving the tablets - then carving their language in stone, chipping in the gypsum stone the cuneiform script with an unbelievable care, art, perfection, so many centuries ago.

Fingers, my hand, centuries later, my mind, very far from Assyria, now a "dead" civilization, touching the written language, knowing the written language in the cool gypsum stone - in the shadowy vestibule of the Maine college museum. The physical art of language, of ephemeral speech, words realized in stone - I touched this "venerable" cuneiform lightly with my fingers. My "sacred" language I touched, the first human language, written, this knowledge in my mind, fingers on stone.

voices. To be drawn out of my self by their femininity - to be in touch

in the beginning, boy, the beautiful slow
    line, a restrained human hand drawing
   human bodies and faces, Michelangelo,
Raphael and Leonardo - but then Cezanne and Picasso for.

          Strike!   (Yeah I'm a goddman millworker & it was
                        Lucky Hotham sitting on his stool
                        at the Rewinders, pushing buttons
                        to move the finished, coated rolls
                        down the conveyer belt to the kickers
              who said "Who the hell you guys kiddin' Fallon!
                        That stuff you guys write ain't poetry an'
                                                you know it!" in
                    the noise of the rewinders/supercalenders
WE WENT ON STRIKE AGAINST BOISE CASCADE
JUNE 30TH MIDNITE LOCAL 900 PAPERWORKERS
   LEFT THE MILL. PICKET LINES WERE SET UP
OUTSIDE THE GATES & ANGRY PAPERMAKERS CURSED
THE SALARIED WORKERS DRIVING OUT THE LOWER GATE
SPITTING ON WINDSHIELDS & POUNDING HOODS
    DOORS, THREATENING THE ENEMY BOISE CASCADE
    FISTS & "THE FINGER" THRUST INTO
          FAMILIAR HUMAN FACES BEHIND
                    GLASS

  in the Rumford night, orange lights glare THE PAPER MILL
      in the parking lot, curses   curses
  IN THE PARKING LOT NOISE!   shouted
                and i was angry with Jackie/divorced always
HATED -   HATRED!   CUT THE CONTRACT IN HALF
                  "YOU WANNA BUST THE UNION BASTARDS!"

with my masculinity, sexuality, my creativity, surrounded by these thre

1946

the boy
  an awareness, a sensitivity
    to
        his soul

                  and, to the world
                  around the soul.
        from a young
          age, child very small,
          a heightened
                    sensitivity to the soul,
                and its need

to its fineness,
its beauty, perfection, inside himself, his
relation to his soul known
                        very young,
                        untaught
      of the fineness - aware, especially

  when the fineness, his sensitivity
                        was violated,
                          his soul
    violated, his heightened
      awareness
            of the perfection
            violated;
                  the necessities
                        of his soul
        with-held
            from the soul,
      then a heightened necessity
                        for his fullness
  then unfulfilled: emptiness, inside,

women. Gentle voices, voices more gentle than a man's, I hear through

                                        a terror
        of the unfulfillment, his soul's
                                            fullness,
    life, emptied,
        threatened his soul's life - he, was

    in
            danger, if the soul was not fulfilled:
        aware, even, the little boy.
                                        the life
        of his soul a reality
                    to him, inside him self, the
                size of himself in its awareness
        when fully alive, moving
                            to its nature,
        its work, necessity: when, stilled, danger,
            for himself, when the soul
                                    was not working
            in reality - stopped up, from
                            the work
        to be, It-self.   The soul, with
                            a life of its own
                    inside, himself, independent,
                                        necessary

                                                to be
            the little boy...   separate, not
                            separated
                                is its

                                reality
        he
            was aware
                without training, (discouraged
                            by many, ignored, the soul,

    the night in the Lab. Look at the women, moving past me, testing paper

his soul, by others, not

spoken of

as reality, in himself
nor, did he speak of his soul
as it existed

to anyone, other human
beings,
even though, it existed
in himself
reality.) Reality

nature
with himself and his soul, his life, his
wholeness a separateness, his awareness

of the duality, child, within himself,
fluctuating

in and
out
of wholeness, the soul's
fulfillment
and urgency

as life was not as urgent, in need - outside,
outside

the world, objects, human activities, human relations,
but not the soul

except
somewhere

he was aware   of a relation   to his soul,
outside himself,   and
communicating with his soul   which
he could not define, very easily

look at the lines of hips, of breasts, the "easy" line of their hips and

                    interrupted the flow
between his soul, and its awareness of the other
                        which communicated to his

soul,   a bodiless, unnamed

                        movement, "life" between
his soul and that other of which
                    he was aware, and, by which he
was measured   his soul -   aware of, yet not
                            aware of
                                the place
            this communication
                    emanated
                            from:
gave more reality to his soul,
   "substance" to his soul
                    this unnamed,
                        awareness of him, his soul.
            the boy would not let go
of his soul, or the other

        even when other human beings denied
        the reality...
                    existence, for
                        the boy, as
            the mother, automobile,
                    although denied
            a place in the every day
            world -

        the boy knew the soul's "matter" and
its every day work - the soul
        would not be denied
                in him   or through him.....

their breasts remain in my mind, form a continuous movement of "easy"

the boy   in the slow life of the soul
the world outside
                    is forgotten, action
is forgotten, action, outside the soul, and is
        remembered
                    only
                        as necessary to
                    his soul's
            life
                in itself, fully in
                            itself, with

                a "stillness", his own,
                            "quietness"
undisturbed -
            the soul drawing
        on its "stillness", his soul

        "quiet" always, enveloping
        memory of his life,
                the world outside

                        the soul,
                            interior
                                life
        drawing life outside within itself
        slowly, as necessary, and re-energizing

        the life outside
            with his soul, a fullness
                    of existential life creation in
        reality: duality,
                    unified, in
            his

lines in my mind throughout the night, a continuous movement of sinuous

soul, from the unnamed outside himself
all energized, motion, objects, human

realities, unified
by the relation of his soul
with "the outside"

beyond himself,
transcending his soul,
his own soul
transcending
his self, drawing from his self
action,
his
vitality, continuous, he was recreated
with his soul
and the unnamed
relation
of the "stillness" - unnamed silence - in
his awareness
with his soul,
sensitivity to
his
unnamed relation
in world
life, human relations, objects
"sensitized"
with
his soul
and
the unnamed communion
to
essences,
magnified
in the soul's life,

lines, resourceful lines, catalyzing my sexuality, my creativity, my de

necessity, for life, objects
and
human relations
transcended but transmogrified
through his soul and its
relation
with the silence
for a reality
understood
in his

awareness
clearly
despite its continuous motion,
despite his continuous
movement in time,
held by his soul
thoroughly in stillness
in his own "quiet" fullness,
whole
of soul, perfect movement in
silence from the unnamed
relation outside
his self - nurtured,
by
green trees, by water flowing,
and, so nurtured by sky and
winter
snow,
birds flying, or calling,
and the cat in the yard, rain
falling
lightly, a human child
walking -

for the continuous movement of women's bodies...I see the bounty of nature,

her face - love's
communion with
his physical self
and hers, soul,

she pregnant - relations with
his soul,

relation to the unnamed outside, a
communion of reality - unspoken

by others around
him, seriously - yet,

the afternoon crickets fill the air
with their continuous natural sounding -
and, it is ignored
as reality, as "knowledge"
for his soul
except by himself
who needs the soul's existence
and
understanding
(the sacrifice
for the soul)
his
soul
to be in understanding,
communication, to be

aware
of its
own whole and the whole of the unnamed, its life a reality
undeniable

in the Lab, 11-7 at night, as the three women move around in front of

                  for him alone,
             relative to
                      objects and human
                           relations, continuously,
                     vitally
               for
                   the suffusing "silence"

         in itself, and in the willow
             on the front lawn

                  - the words in his mind
                    a reality: sacred,
within his soul

           -   s e e n .

     drawn
        then, the boy of
          ten, in the face
                 of an old woman -
         Mrs. Grey - soul in
    reality, on
     the pink paper quickly
    drawn
        with a pencil - stopped,
     human activity, in his soul

             and on the paper
               with a pencil,
               naturally

"promoting" nature, "advertising" creation, with their gentle words, and as usual

there

the art making life, soul made, the unnamed
relation drawing
the woman out

automatically from
its soul, boy,
creation from his self

the necessary
act of the soul in perfection only -

his soul a reality on the pink paper
and everyone knew, indistinctly

- the soul clear in him - (not clearly
aware of the soul) -

from the drawing, reality

they knew
however indistinctly, and agreed, the soul's
existence in their astonishment, recognition, of that drawn

soul   there.   a child's awareness was the reality
for everyone

(the [his] soul)   and
its
relation   explicit
spirituality
clear   .

voices, in my mind, becoming part of my self, their gentle voices in my

parturition:

(rare, delicate

beyond/and human)

his

soul   "sight"

within the boy, his reality in Auburn, parturition

1956 - notebook: "Why does human hatred exist?"

At the North Star Coater, I had let the Clay Filter System
overflow three times. I'd been under the Coater reading.
"Gump" Bernard sent me back to Personnel with a note: Don't
send this man back to me again. I didn't care; I wasn't
really interested in working anyway. Personnel sent me to
the Beater Room where I read and slept. I didn't care about
making paper at the Oxford. Anyway, everyone read and slept
in the mill. What was the big deal about "Gump" Bernard?

1956 - notebook: "Chaos - chaos - chaos - why? I do not
understand this..."

natural self, resonant, stirring the "dull beast" in my self to creation...

*I hate society: I despise conformity. I desire to destroy
this conformity - I am criminal. I hate, poetry. (I hate it.)
I will create.. I am criminal.*

& "Sounding"

NO LONGER IN THE PAPER MILL AT WORK THE PAPER MILL A
REALITY EFFECTING ME...AT THE END OF TWO DAYS AWAY FROM
THE PAPER MILL THE CONSCIOUS THOUGHT OF THE PAPER MILL
BEGINS TO FADE...CONSCIOUS THOUGHT OF THE PAPER MILL
BEGINS TO FADE WHICH DOESN'T MEAN THAT THE PAPER MILL
IS FORGOTTEN, THE TENSION CREATED BY WORK AT THE PAPER
MILL BEGINS TO DISAPPEAR FROM MY BODY FROM MY MIND
THE TENSION DOES NOT DISAPPEAR FROM MY UNCONSCIOUS...
THE PAPER MILL, THE PAPER MILL, STILL EXISTS IN MY BODY
AND IN MY THOUGHT...THE NON-HUMAN NOISE, THE NON-HUMAN
SPEED THE PRESSURE ON THE HUMAN BODY AND MIND, THE FORM
OF NON-HUMAN MOVEMENT - THE NON-HUMAN PROCEDURES BETWEEN
HUMAN BEINGS EXIST CONTINUOUSLY IN MY UNCONSCIOUS MIND
AFTER TWO WEEKS VACATION FROM THE PAPER MILL...OUTSIDE
        THE PAPER MILL, MY BODY, MIND, IS STILL ENVELOPED BY
THE RHYTHM OF THE PAPER MILL...THE PAPER MILL APPEARS
AGAIN IN MY CONSCIOUS THOUGHT AFTER TWO WEEKS VACATION
AWAY FROM THE MILL I CANNOT FORGET THE PAPER MILL, I
CANNOT FORGET EVEN AFTER TWO WEEKS OUTSIDE THE PAPER
MILL THE PAPER MILL, EVEN WHEN THE MILL HAS FADED FROM
MY CONSCIOUS THOUGHT AFTER TWO DAYS THE PAPER MILL RETURNS
TO MY CONSCIOUS MIND THEN, THE NON-HUMAN NOISE A REALITY
IN MY CONSCIOUS MIND EVEN AFTER TWO WEEKS...I THINK OF
THE PAPER MILL...THE NON-HUMAN...VIBRATION OF THE CEMENT

And I am able to clearly feel the women around me, feel the women in my

FLOOR UNDERNEATH MY BODY, I AM SHAKEN BY THE NOISE VIBRATING
THE AIR, VIBRATING THE BUILDING, VIBRATING THE FLOOR
WITH THE FORCE OF THE MACHINES' MOVEMENT, THE PAPER MILL
IS IN CONTINUOUS MOVEMENT I AM IN CONTINUOUS MOVEMENT
WHEN I AM IN THE MILL...I EXIST IN THE REALITY OF THE
PAPER MILL...I EXIST IN THE REALITY OF THE PAPER MILL'S
NON-HUMAN REALITY...SPEED SPEED CONTINUOUS SPEED EXISTS
AND MOVEMENT, THE FORCE OF THE MOVING MACHINERY, TWO
WEEKS OUTSIDE THE PAPER MILL, THE NOISE, SPEED, FORCE,
CONTINUOUS
MOVEMENT EXISTS, THE HARD NOISE, THE HARD SPEED, THE
CONSCIOUS THOUGHT...AFTER TWO DAYS I BEGAN TO FORGET
THE PAPER MILL, TWO WEEKS LATER I BEGAN TO REMEMBER,
FROM MY UNCONSCIOUS THOUGHT, THE MOVEMENT OF THE MACHINES
EXISTING IN MY CONSCIOUS MIND...THE SHOUTED WORDS THE
SHOUTED WORDS IN MY EAR...THE PAPER MILL, MOVEMENT AND
SPEED OF MACHINERY, MOTORS, IN MY MIND, THE FORCE ON
MY BODY, IN MY BODY, HARDNESS, EXISTS, THE PAPER MILL
CREATES A STIFFNESS IN MY BODY, A TENSION, A FEAR IN
MY MIND, IN MY BODY, A HARDNESS...HATE...I AM ABLE TO
REMEMBER THE HATE INSIDE THE PAPER MILL, CURSES, MY PERSON
BUFFETED BY SOUND, HARD SOUND...I THINK...STIFF, STIFF...
IRON STEEL CEMENT MOVEMENT SPEED VIBRATION AROUND
MYSELF, MY PERSONAL SELF...THE NON-HUMAN PROCEDURES,
NUMBERS, THE NUMBERS, PRODUCTION NUMBERS, MOVE MOVE

mind, clearly, I am "swimming" in the "waves" emanating from the women's

179

Title of this recording `GALLERY` – *Oliver Lake*

Comments *Very very good jazz. Better than recent Murray, Pullen music I've bought.*

How did this album come to your attention? *Downbeat magaz review.*

Bought at *Amadeus, Portland, Maine – 2/28/87*

Mail to: GRAMAVISION RECORDS
          260 West Broadway, Dep't MO
          New York, NY 10013

Dear Record Buyer:

Thank you for adding this recording to your library. We hope you
will enjoy it for years to come. We appreciate the time you take
to send us your comments. They are extremely helpful to us and
our artists.

Sincerely,
Gramavision Records

flesh, spirituality, as they move, walk around the Lab, walk around me

2.

denise levertov has zeroed in on the major creative impulse in
            20th century literature: the inventor is our archetype,
she has groped toward a new terminology for the inventor and her
        3 writer-types in (a further definition) form inventors for
thoughts feelings & perceptions/formless writers ignoring sonic
&rhythmic patterns/organic writers seeking forms peculiar to
   particular thoughts feelings & perceptions   seek to define the
                                  intellectuals who search for
& invent new literary forms; paralleling technological,science's
invention   EZRA POUND OUTLINED UNIVERSAL LITERARY TYPES IN HIS
ABC OF READING yet in practice CANTOS; violated his classicism, with
collage style deSTRUCTION OF POETRYINTHEOLDSENSE A PSYCHOLO
GIC   disorientation in narrative line, of chaos idea & sensation)
1950 charlie olson wrote verse to be useful had to accept new stance
                  toward reality/itself   it had to recognize
THE POSSIBILITIES OF TYPEWRITER AS TOOL&its spacing,human breath
        in structuring linelength;olsons call for a new
verse to replace inherited LINE STANZA/OVERALL FORM,seminal
direction/Ollie also wrote, begin to examine several forces at
work in pound, williams cummings/discussed freer more inventive
verse   based on this trio
                    BUT OLLIE SO SPOKE IN THE TRADITION OF
POESY, BABY! POINTING AWAY FROM POETRY BABY! as did levertov as
did levertov with her new criticial definitions

speaking of the line length in a new general terminology, different
from that terminology used in traditional prosody traditional
                                                    prosody/
DEFINING THE LINE BREAK WITH NEW AGE'S THOUGHT-DIRECTION
with a THINKING-FEELING terminology   the recording of
   the minds movement in words on-the-page or THE FIELD pointing
(the closed, contained quality of such traditional forms has less in
   relation to relativistic sense/that are more EXPLORATORY -)   SHE
SAID

he brightly lighted room, "touching" me with their femininity, with their

3.

this is the experiment - invent - we are involved in
the experiment - the goal is to change history - invent - begin,
    again: we must absorb,naturally,changes naturally,
 of living language sure,

                                                    Drive

                              Miles Davis goes electric

                                                    Drive
                              Miles Davis goes electric

Flight to the moon, a landing, and photos of the earth in
                                                    space.

                                                    DRIVE
                              Miles Davis goes electric
Flight to the moon, a landing, and photos of the earth in
                                                    space.

                                                    DRIVE
                              "Tune in, turn on, drop out!"

                                                    DRIVE
"There's reason to believe Oswald killed Kennedy alone..."

                    (TO BE CONTINUED   )

SUPPLEMENT TO
THE MAN ON THE MOON

*   *   *

FROM
THE PIONEERS BABY!

An Essay Concerning the Past,
Present & Future of Literature

TOM FALLON

From the Pioneers Baby!

Tom Fallon

> "Time is the greatest innovator."
> Francis Bacon

Preface

The first step on the road to my discovery of a new literary category was Ezra Pound's challenging ABC OF READING; next, T. S. Eliot and James Joyce. The innovation of the Sixties' off-off Broadway theater William Carlos Williams' entire work - and at the end of the line came Dick Higgins Then, my mind was ready for Marianne Moore's startling declaration.

1.

Denise Levertov presented 3 writer types in her essay, "A Further Definition":

1) Form Inventors for Thoughts, Feelings & Perceptions W/out Form
2) Formless Writers Ignoring Sonic & Rhythmic Patterns
3) Organic Writers Seeking Forms Peculiar to Particular Thoughts, Feelings & Perceptions

And while Ole Ez Pound classified 6 universal writer types in his AEC OF READING - Inventors, Masters, Dilutors, Good Writers, Belle Lettrists, & Craze Starters - Levertov's 3 apply specifically to our age as writers search for & invent new literary forms paralleling the new technological inventions & scientific discoveries.

(Yeah, in practice, Ole Ez violated the universality principle related by his 6 writer classes, he waz, very much, the mawdern - hiz CANTOS practically attacked poetry "in the old sense" with a collage style destruction/psychological disorientation favoring a chaos of idea/FORM/ sensation clearly expressing the "human battlefield" in our mawdern times Ba-by!)

OK.

Charles Olson. (1950.) Ollie wrote that verse would be useful if it accepted a new stance toward reality & itself - it must recognize the possibilities of the human breath in structuring the line length - it must find a use for the typewriter & its spacing in line form. His Open- Projective Verse & Field essay, calling for a new verse to replace the inherited line stanza/tradition as well as reconstruction of overall form is a seminal directive to modern inventors in literary/art form.

Ollie saw that we were only beginning to examine the vital forces in the pioneering work of Ole Ez WCW & ee. when he proposed a freer more inventive verse based on this "Big Trio" - as well as - AS WELL AS - pointing beyond them to future literary composition opposing the simple variations in traditional prosody so many depended on for their emotional and intellectual security.

Back to that woman - 1979 - Levertov began to outline the new (exploratory) form Ollie had called for - which many writers practiced by this time - but imperfectly understood - feeling it necessary in the essay - "Technique and Tune-up" - to define the open form which had evolved naturally in our time because very little charting of the territory existed for readers/writers except "in the old sense", in the old (DRIED-up)

terms.

DL discussed line length in a new general terminology different from that used in traditional prosody - defined the line break with a "thinking-feeling" terminology - the recording of the human mind's movement through words on the page - or "the field" - illustrating the new mind-stance which existed in the
verse composition of our age.

Speaking
of line indentation and the use of the margin Levertov defined the page "field" and writing thereon as the "score" of the "thinking-feeling" mind which provided an emotional graph in words on "the field" - her definitions in the essay seek to outline in general terms the techniques of the 3 literary classes presented in "A Further Definition" - to fill the gap in modern literary criticism & definition - she groped toward a new terminology rooted in the modern exploration of form.

"The closed, contained quality of such (traditional) forms," she wrote in 'On the Function of the Line', "has less relation to the relativistic

sense of life which unavoidably prevails in the late 20th Century than
modes that are more exploratory/open-minded," she wrote striving to
define the inventive direction of modern literary form.
So be it. Invention. The inventor expresses the vital creative
(literary) direction of the mawdern world, Baby! That seems to be
the gist of the situation -

2.

I needed a photo of Marianne Moore, sweet Marianne, which I
could Xerox for elementary and secondary school poetry workshops. I
had photos of Walt Whitman and William Carlos Williams but wanted
Sweet Marianne because I felt her grandmotherly looks would appeal
to youngsters.
I sent to the Maine State Library for books - what can a
"one-horse" town like Rumford have in its library? - when I received
the books via mail I found no photo I could use - so I put the books
up on the shelf uninterested in reading them but unwilling to return
them because of my expense.
A week later I took Sweet Marianne's books down to return them
to the state library - then decided to skim through them rather than
completely waste my mailing expense.
I was disgusted with the first Sweet Marianne essay because it was
littered with quotes - I began another only to find the same "junk
trip" - thumbed through the book and decided she couldn't possibly
ruin an interview - Donald Hall's interview for the Paris Review - I
read the questions and her answers until I came to this statement -

"I disliked the word 'poetry' for any but Chaucer or
Shakespeare or Dante. I do not now feel quite my original
hostility to the word, since it is a convenient almost unavoidable
term for the thing (although hardly for me - my observations,
experiments in rhythm, or exercises in composition) What I
write, as I have said before, could only be called poetry because
there is no other category in which to put it.

(Oh Jesus!) "What I write as I have said before could only be
called poetry because there is no other category in which to put it."
I was stunned by that revolutionary sentence - I knew immediately

that I was not a poet
    (Jesus, Jesus, Sweet Marianne, do you know what you thought when
you uttered those words? - and not for the first time!) - I saw them
in an old Life
magazine too - I understood IMMEDIATELY THAT NOT ONLY WAS I NOT
WRITING POETRY BUT OTHERS WHO FELT THEY WERE WRITING POETRY
WERE NOT WRITING POETRY EITHER - I was stunned intellectually -
here was the revelatory truth - the creative truth - I had been
searching for through the years of working/wandering search in
literary form - creating off-beat forms in plays fiction finally "poetry"
- some termed simply form for want of a better word because I felt
they were not poetry but I didn't know what they were -
                & look at all those wierd literary forms that were
being created termed poetry that
could only be termed poetry because there was NO OTHER CATEGORY
FOR THEM - no one had taken the risk - BUT SWEET MARIANNE - !
    & she said "there is no other category in which to put it" -
opening a door in the mind, Little Tommy's door/mind - whoosh Air!
No poetry - need another form, another category - (Jesus, Jesus,
Marianne, Sweet Marianne - Sweet Grandmotherly Marianne, how the
hell could you? Didn't you know you were upsetting an old
applecart?)
    (I've already said I was stunned.) OK. Then I began to conduct
research to prove or disprove this theory of Sweet Marianne's -
which I did feel to be an aesthetic/creative truth - I read
essays/criticism from different literary periods and compared many
different traditional poems with many different modern poems - with
many poems I didn't feel were poems - to discover if a new literary
form had come into existence as the sweet unrevolutionary-looking
little old lady had suggested so clearly in her interview - yeah.
    And what did I find - I found that a new literary category had
not been posited but had been suggested by other writers - after
reading essays and criticism in the plastic arts - I found that other
artistic categories had been created in the plastic arts for new
invented forms - I found that an obvious literary/artistic revolution -
had taken place in the century that had not been fully realized - I
found that the only move left was to take the risk and place a term
in the marketplace of ideas -

I did. What the hell! (What do you think Ez?) This act was in the
mawdern tradition.

Sweet, Sweet, Marianne Moore! Moving the history of the mind –
yeah! "Make it new." "No ideas but in things." "I disliked the
word poetry..."

Three

Questions   Questions.
    The question. Search   The searchers, the pioneers, of our time –
exploring the world – and ideas, culture, etc   The question is the
archetypal – intellectual – word equation of our century – "spiritual"
declaration, the question: exploration –

    Is free verse the poetry of our age?

    What is the definition of free verse?   (My definition of free
        verse)
    What, objectively, is free verse?
    Investigate.

    What writer began free verse?
    Milton? Wordsworth? Whitman?
    Did free verse have its origin in the 19th century? Or earlier?
    Did it begin in the US? France? England?

    What social circumstances existed during the change from verse
        to free verse?
    Political revolution? Industrial revolution? Democracy?
    What was the literary situation which led to the origin of free
        verse? *Research this*

    Demonstrate the evolution of free verse with "specimens".

    What did Beaudelaire mean when he wrote in his intro to Paris
    Spleen

        "Which one of us, in his moments of ambition, has not
        dreamed of the miracle of a poetic prose, musical, without
        rhythm or without rhyme, supple enough and rugged enough
        to adapt itself to the lyrical impulses of the soul, the
        undulations of reverie, the jibes of conscience?

In what direction was he pointing?

How do free verse and the prose-poem relate?
What is a prose-poem? (The accepted definition))
Study the prose-poem for yourself. Define it.
Is the prose-poem poetry? It isn't termed either prose or
   poetry...
What is a prose-poem?

How many poetic techniques can be eliminated from a prose-poem
   - while still maintaining
the integrity of its prose-poem nature?
Shouldn't this form have been given a new label rather than the
makeshift term "prose-poem"?
Could the prose-poem be termed "free verse" rather than
"prose-poem"?

What's organic verse?
Is it a sub-category of free verse?
What is the last poetic technique to be eliminated from free
      verse?   Is free verse, with only one poetic technique,
metaphor, still poetry?

Are some kinds of free verse closer to poetry than others -
         should then still be termed poetry - others more distant,
         with less or no poetic techniques except *through a
stretch of imagination*, so shouldn't be termed poetry?

Sonic and rhythmic patterning in free verse - is this "diluted"
· poetry?
Free verse?
Unconscious sonic and rhythmic patterning?
Investigate how many writers don't attend to prosody except by
"accident" - ?

Dactyllic rhythm in free verse?
Not conscious prosody, dactyllic measure...
Investigate the point

Whitman: "I have never given any study merely to expression it has
never

appealed to me as a thing valuable in itself..." and,   "What I am
after is the content not the music of words. Perhaps music happens –
it does no harm."
        Does this point out that Whitman paid no attention to technique,
was not only careless of it, but tried to ignore it to focus on his
subject alone?
Did he pay attention to sonic and rhythmic patterning?
Read the 1955 *Leaves of Grass*.

        GINSBERG – The question is how to figure out where
to break a line.
Since ("New York to Fran") was written down a page, the page
determines
the length of line...if I have a big enough notebook, it's a long line...
If it's a little pocket notebook that you stick in your back pocket
then
you tend to have smaller, choppier lines... My basic measure is a unit
of thought...
                                        and

Actually, it is a kind of natural speech rhythm that comes when
you are speaking slowly, interestedly, to a friend. With the kind
of breaks that are hesitancies waiting for the next thought to
articulate itself...

How, does this working habit of AG relate to poetic technique?
        Sonic and rhythmic patterning?
        Free verse?

Poetry...

        Whitman/Ginsberg's compositional experience parallels my own in
some respects – do I write poetry? Free verse?
INVESTIGATE YOUR WRITING FORM

        Is there a point
                        where what we call free verse
                                                no longer
remains
        poetry?
Free – verse – is it possible for verse to be free verse and still be

labeled verse?
      Poetry? Poetry?
Investigate
specimens of free verse under a microscope.

   What is verse?

   Poetry -   what is poetry?
   Collect specimens of poems.
   Collect definitions of poems.
   Examine specimens of poems under a microscope.

   Has the definition of poetry been broadened to include any literary
form
which isn't prose?
      Just a minute - has the poetry category. been extended to include
      new, invented, literary forms, which aren't prose, and aren't
poetry?
         Should there be another literary category for literary forms
falling outside poetry and prose?

OKAY! What invented literary forms of the 20th Century shouldn't be

   categorized as poetry? *Collect specimens of these.*

   INVESTIGATE ‹radical› 20th Century forms listed in the poetry
   category   - for want of an existing term - such as concrete
poetry, sound poetry, text art, collage, video poetry, performance
poetry, etc.

      Collect specimens to analyse poetic and non-poetic techniques.

      What is "anti-poetry"?
      Should another term be used for the anti-poem?

What does it mean when a film is termed "poetic" by critics?

What does it mean when a novel is labeled "poetic" by critics?

Finnegan's Wake?
Poetry - poetry?
What, Ezra Pound's Cantos - say it!
Paterson?

  What did Gertrude Stein write?
   Category...?

THE FRENCH NOUVEAU ROMAN? Borges? Investigate literary form.

  Gather specimens for analysis Observe without bias. (Remain
severely objective, remember you have that "necessary" baggage of
emotional/intellectual security for combat in your mind, baby!) Collect
data
on the nature of the specimens.
No conclusion should be reached until you have conducted research.

Question poetry, non-poetry, prose, as seriously as you question the
words of politicians and used-car salesmen.

                              4.

  Well, let's drop the new literary theory on you so you can chew
it over at the next university cocktail party or book publishing event
you ain't gonna do it over a beer at the neighborhood beer joint on
Main St. or while you're having your oil changed at Mobil I know
that!
  We have the present literary categories poetry and prose
under the "Theory of Historical Literary Form" amended, extended,
by my - (with the stimulation/agitation of the literary pioneers of our
century) new literary theory the "Theory of Creative Literary
Form"
  The new theory emphasizes possibility creativity open, new
forms, rather than the closed forms of the traditional poetry and
prose categories. Emphasizes the possibility for creating new forms
and new categories in literature empasizes actually the necessity for
the creation of new literary forms/categories as human consciousness is
expanded/effected by the extension of human knowledge/experience
about the world and life as human consciousness is being

expanded/effected/exploded now in our intellectual history
                        The creative explosion   here and now   free
creation
exploration of aesthetic forms   questioning aesthetic form   undermining
aesthetic forms   20th century, is from the plastic arts/literary
pioneers yes
as is the reality of human life today/before in history time days, so
that the "Theory of Creative Literary Form" MAKES IT POSSIBLE FOR
FREE
CREATION TO EXIST AS A REALITY (protects free exploration)

so while I posit a new literary category today   charteng   (charting) it
is
NOW possible to replace charteng in the future   when necessary &
that
            necessity will exist one day in the future   with a new

                                                literary category
                            A NEW LITERARY CATEGORY
TO
     make free creation possible   poetry & prose are not the last
word
in literary categories. Charteng is not the last word in a literary
category, but the "Theory of Creative Literary Form" is the last word
in
literary theories because it opens up the possibility for all new
                                                    literary
categories as
necessary to human intellectual/spiritual evolution & growth which are
now taking place   have over the past century   have with the
Renaissance   have with 5th century Greece   creative growth
exploding

in the 20th century & now into the 21st century yeah! So we have a
new
literary theory & new literary category   yes I listen to jazz/that
new musical form of the 20th century almost daily

This is the end of this essay on creative exploration   "Watcha thinkin

Ez?" (We did it!) "You a bad mutha, Ezra! You a real bad
mutha!" (We did it!)

A Summary Bibliography

The proposition for a new literary category different from poetry and
prose has been presented via essays and reviews in many literary
magazines and books.

Charles Olson, Wallace Stevens, James Laughlin, Bill Knott, Marianne
Hauser and others have pointed to this possibility. And the concept is
clearly suggested in the explorations, discoveries and inventions of Ezra
Pound, T. S. Eliot, Gertrude Stein, James Joyce, William Carlos Williams,
e. e. cummings, Dick Higgins, Richard Kostelanetz, Denise Levertov, John
Ashbery, etc.

The following bibliography culled from my research on the subject is
not exhaustive but will give the reader or scholar an awareness of this
direction in modern literature. An objective, comparative analysis of
traditional prose and modern prose, traditional poetry and modern poetry,
on a one-to-one specimen basis, will provide more proof for the Theory of
Creative (Literary) Form in the 20th Century.

The Marianne Moore Reader. The Paris Review Interview with Donald Hall.
   (Viking Press, NY, 1961).
"American Book Review", Nov/Dec 1980. Review of Harriet Zinnes ENTROPISMS
   by Marianne Hauser.
The American Moment by Geoffrey Thurley. P 119. (St. Martin's Press).
Selected Writings of Charles Olson, edited by Robert Creeley. "Projective
   Verse" essay. (New Directions).
Composed on the Tongue, Allen Ginsberg, edited by Donald Allen. "Improvised
   Poetics: essay-interview (Grey Fox Press, Bolinas, CA)
foew&ombwhnw, by Dick Higgins. Essays on intermedia. (Something Else
   Press, Barrytown, NY).
Imaginations, by William Carlos Williams "Spring and All". (New Directions).
Art News, May 1980, article by Paul Gardner about Shusaku Arakawa
Encyclopedia of Poetry and Poetics, edited by Alex Preminger. (Princeton
   U. Press) See "Verse and Prose".
Possibilities of Poetry, edited by Richard Kostelanetz. (Dell, NY, 1970).
Wordsand, by Richard Kostelanetz. (RK Editions)
"American Poetry Review", Nov/Dec 1980. Robert Miklitsch's "Ut Pictura
   Poesis: Reduction and Contemporary American Painting and Poetry".
The New Walt Whitman Handbook, edited by Gay Wilson Allen (NYU Press)
Endless Life. by Lawrence Ferlinghetti "Modern Poetry is Prose" (New
   Directions)
Interview with William Carlos Williams, edited by Linda Wagner The 3
   interviews (New Directions)
The Making of Jazz, by James Lincoln Collier (A Delta Book, Dell Publishing
   Co., NY, 1978).
The Death of Tragedy, by George Steiner. (Faber & Faber, London).

APPENDIX

Many intellectuals have approached the subject of revolutionary literary form in the 20th Century, suggesting that new categories might be necessary to define the innovations of the time. Usually, however, they backed away from the final "leap of the imagination" - their focus was not on understanding that new literary categories were necessary so much as in creating new forms to fill that as yet unnamed category. I have been left with the discovery of the new literary category as others have discovered new categories in the other arts of our revolutionary time.

The following quotations will introduce you to a few of those who have entertained the subject of new artistic or literary categories:

"Whether 'Einstein' or any of Glass' operas is a perennial, whether they are operas at all, for that matter, are questions that have driven critics into warring sectarian camps for a dozen years.
                              Anthony Tommasini, Boston Globe, May 15, 1988

"Some observers, including Glass himself in the beginning, were reluctant to call his major theater pieces 'operas'. Director and scenarist Robert Wilson, Glass' first and most frequent collaborator, used the word opera in its original sense, meaning 'works', that is, a theater spectacle involving multiple genres: music, visuals, movement, speech. Other designations - 'music-theater work', 'music-visual work', 'tableau opera' - were tried on, but opera won out. 'The word "opera" wouldn't be good if it gave people the wrong idea,' Glass says, 'but people who come to a Philip Glass opera know they're not going to see singers in period costumes telling love stories in foreign languages. The battle to reclaim the word has been won.

'Of course, when we were creating "Einstein", the tradition of opera was never an idea for Bob Wilson and me,' Glass says: 'actually, the tradition of opera we thought best forgotten. I have nothing against the Italian tradition. It's given us hundreds, well, let's say, dozens, of masterpieces. But for anyone who has sat at the feet of artists like Jasper Johns, John Cage, Merce Cunningham, Julian Beck, the whole generation that formed the contemporary aesthetic, the tradition of opera, especially as it has been continued by composers like Menotti, Floyd, Argento, Robert Ward, simply doesn't have anything to say. It doesn't speak to me in an authentically modern voice.   Anthony Tommasini, Boston Globe, May 15, 1988

"For THE MECHANISM OF MEANING, Arakawa is constructing a series of several hundred 'panels' (he doesn't call them paintings) that will be a 'model, a catalogue of the mind'.   Art News, May 1980

"I can see why you propose a new name for what we are doing. Whatever it is, it sometimes seems useful to give it a new name to separate it from some of the tedious examples of what is generally called poetry.
                              Personal letter from David Antin, 1980

"I disliked the word 'poetry' for any but Chaucer or Shakespeare or Dante. I do not now feel quite my original hostility to the word, since it is a convenient almost unavoidable term for the thing (although hardly for me - my observations, experiments in rhythm, or exercises in composition). What I write, as I have said before, could only be called poetry because there is no other category in which to put it.
                    Donald Hall Paris Review interview with Marianne Moore

"I have referred to ENTROPISMS as prose poems, with some reluctance. Others have employed the term. James Laughlin who originally published the first half of the book in his anthology 27, states that 'ENTROPISMS are an important evolution of the prose poem as a literary form.' The poet Bill Knott suspects the form to be a new form, one that falls between verse and prose poem (which many are writing so badly, he adds in parenthesis.) But what are we to call that new form Or do we need a label? / Indeed, Harriet Zinnes' art does not seem to fit any label.
                    Marianne Hauser, The American Book Review, Nov/Dec 1980

Good luck with seeing into and trying to charting the elusive muse…awhile back I did a minor paper after a major research effort, trying to define the difference between old and new poetry, and attempting to explain what 'modern poetry' means Conclusion: poetry died some time ago.
                                    D.A. Anderson, personal letter

"All the ways and means we have of writing just go to prove that no one has yet discovered the one best way.   William Carlos Williams

"For I confront peace, security, and all the settled laws, to unsettle them.   Walt Whitman, LEAVES OF GRASS

"I once wrote a few works about 6 years ago, in a different structural capacity than either prose or poetry, and called it proto (as a generic term) The work itself was a cross between a poem and a novel and the individual term for it was poemel. I followed that 100-pager with a 30-pager termed poemella…Anyway, the idea of charting must be exciting to you To be able to rename 'poetry'. I've never heard of it being attempted That in itself is a literary happening…
                                    Dave Morice, personal letter

"The stance involves, for example, a change beyond, and larger than, the technical, and may, the way things look, lead to new poetics and to new concepts   Charles Olson, "Projective Verse"

"Though I once said that my creative work made me 'a poet', I now speak of myself as an 'artist and writer', wishing there were in English a single term that combined the two. 'Maker' might be more appropriate, its modesty notwithstanding. Perhaps the work is ultimately about the

LITERATURE

After PATERSON, after the CANTOS, after MAXIMUS,
after "A", comes THE MAN ON THE MOON, a synthesis
of 20th Century literary innovation.

All the ways and means we have of
writing just go to prove that no one has
yet discovered the one best way.
William Carlos Williams

The stance involves, for example, a
change beyond, and larger than, the
technical, and may, the way things look,
lead to new poetics and to new
concepts...
Charles Olson

What I write, as I have said before, could
only be called poetry because there is
no other category...
Marianne Moore

COVER
*Earth-view from Apollo 8 as the spacecraft rises from
behind the moon. NASA Photo.*

A TRANSITION BOOK   ISBN 0-9616146-3-3